The Urban Housing Manual

The Urban Housing Manual
Making Regulatory Frameworks Work for the Poor

Geoffrey Payne and Michael Majale

London • Sterling, VA

First published by Earthscan in the UK and USA in 2004

ISBN: 1-84407-148-0

Typesetting by MapSet Ltd, Gateshead, UK
Printed and bound in the UK by Cromwell Press Ltd
Cover design by Anthony Waters
Illustrations © Ripin Kalra

For a full list of publications please contact:
Earthscan
8–12 Camden High Street
London, NW1 0JH, UK
Tel: +44 (0)20 7387 8558
Fax: +44 (0)20 7387 8998
Email: earthinfo@earthscan.co.uk
Web: **www.earthscan.co.uk**

22883 Quicksilver Drive, Sterling, VA 20166-2012, USA

Earthscan publishes in association with WWF-UK and the International Institute for Environment
and Development

A catalogue record for this book is available from the British Library

Library of Congress Cataloging-in-Publication Data

Payne, Geoffrey K.
    The urban housing manual : making regulatory frameworks work for the poor / Geoffrey
Payne and Michael Majale.
        p. cm.
    Includes bibliographical references and index.
    ISBN 1-84407-148-0 (pbk.)
    1. Urban poor—Housing—Government policy—Developing countries—Handbooks,
manuals, etc. 2. Low-income housing—Government policy—Developing countries—
Handbooks, manuals, etc. 3. Housing policy—Developing countries—Handbooks, manuals,
etc. 4. Squatter settlements—Developing countries—Handbooks, manuals, etc. 5. Slums—
Developing countries—Handbooks, manuals, etc. I. Majale, Michael, 1958–II. Title.

HD7287.96.D44P39 2004
363.5'96942'091724—dc22

                                                                        2004014300

CONTENTS

LIST OF FIGURES, TABLES AND BOXES

FIGURES

TABLES

BOXES

ABOUT THE AUTHORS AND CONTRIBUTORS

Geoffrey Payne is a housing and urban development consultant and principal of Geoffrey Payne and Associates. He specializes in land tenure and property rights, public–private partnerships, housing policy and project design, and has undertaken consultancy, research and training assignments throughout the world. He has published widely and is an associate adviser to the British Council.

Michael Majale was an International Projects Manager with the Intermediate Technology Development Group until August 2003. He is now a lecturer in Overseas Development at the University of Newcastle upon Tyne, where his research interests focus on urbanization and improving the lives and livelihoods of poor people living and working in informal settlements.

CD-ROM EDITOR

Evelyn Tehrani is a gender and international development researcher and an associate at Geoffrey Payne and Associates. She specializes in gender issues related to sustainable livelihoods, rural–urban linkages, land tenure and housing, poverty, and participatory research methods and techniques.

CONTRIBUTORS TO THE CD-ROM OR MANUAL

Uma Adusumilli	Ripin Kalra	Jagath Premakumara
Sundar Burra	Ruşen Keleş	Otto Ruskulis
Sue Cavill	Lusugga Kironde	Theo Schilderman
H M U Chularathna	Stuti Lall	Dilip Shekdar
Andrew Cotton	Lucky Lowe	M Sohail
Fabian Farfan	Michael Majale	Evelyn Tehrani
David Hall	Ruth McLeod	Graham Tipple
K A Jayaratne	Sheela Patel	Kamwati Wango
Rebecca Kabura	Geoffrey Payne	

FOREWORD

From the outset I would like to state that this manual will assist governments in their efforts to specifically attain the Millennium Development Goal 7, Target 11, on improving the lives of at least 100 million slum dwellers by 2020. In addition, countries involved with UN-HABITAT's Global Campaign for Secure Tenure will find this manual a useful tool in developing their slum upgrading frameworks and housing policies. UN-HABITAT wishes to encourage the use of this tool to address the issues of the urban poor.

Following the adoption of the Habitat Agenda, countries throughout the world have now agreed the key features of sustainable policies for human settlements. These provide a sound basis for reducing poverty and improving the economic vitality and living conditions of towns and cities. However, policies are not, in themselves, a sufficient basis for achieving progress on the ground. The ability to successfully implement the Habitat Agenda will be significantly influenced by the regulatory framework of planning regulations, planning standards and administrative procedures by which governments seek to manage the processes of urban development and growth. Where the regulatory framework imposes costs, uncertainty or confusion, investors will be reluctant to take risks, communities will be unable to conform and administrators will be ineffective.

The high and increasing proportion of slums and unauthorized settlements in the towns and cities of developing countries is irrefutable evidence that existing regulatory frameworks have failed to achieve the objective of planned urban growth. In fact, in many instances, more people live outside the formal, planned city than inside it. Slum clearance and relocation programmes have also failed to impose control. It is increasingly clear that the vision of urban development reflected in planning regulations, standards and administrative procedures is out of step with the realities of population growth and widespread poverty. In fact, they are making matters worse rather than better. Current United Nations (UN) estimates indicate that there are 924 million people living in slums and unauthorized settlements, and this is expected to increase to 1500 million by 2015 unless urgent action is taken.

This manual addresses these key issues. It is based on extensive international research undertaken by teams led by Geoffrey Payne and Associates (GPA) and the Intermediate Technology Development Group (ITDG). The ITDG team focused on regulatory guidelines for urban upgrading, while the GPA team addressed ways of increasing access to affordable and legal new housing. The findings of the research confirmed that in most countries, regulatory frameworks need to be revised significantly if governments are to reduce urban poverty and the proportion of households living in slums. In many countries, regulatory requirements are in a language or form local people are unable to understand. In other cases, they are so complex that even the professionals responsible for implementing them are unaware of all the details. In yet others, the procedures involve so many visits to different offices that even professional developers cannot afford the time and costs involved.

Fortunately, the research did not just identify the problems. I know that, thanks to funding by the British Government's Department for International Development (DFID), the teams were able to explore options for change with the relevant authorities. This required negotiations with all the key stakeholders in the public, private and community sectors. Applying the methods developed by the research teams to review existing regulatory frameworks, they were able to identify which specific regulations, standards or procedures represented the key constraints in different locations, and the options that might be adopted to overcome these. It is this experience which forms the basis for the manual. Rather than producing a conventional research report, the editors have produced a practical tool for urban professionals, administrators, development practitioners, community groups and others with which to review and revise regulatory frameworks. I found it useful that, for those interested in having more details or examples of how to undertake reviews or regulatory audits, a CD-Rom is attached to the manual, containing case studies and a wealth of relevant information.

I know also that the manual is being launched as a contribution by DFID to the World Urban Forum in Barcelona in September 2004, which will enjoy the participation of many HABITAT partners. I am sure this will be an opportunity to discuss these issues further.

I trust that users of this manual will find it an effective tool in our collective endeavour to promote universal housing rights

Farouk Tebbal
Chief, Shelter Branch
UN-HABITAT

PREFACE

This publication addresses a subject of critical importance to international efforts to help reduce urban poverty and realize the Millennium Development Goals (MDGs). In an increasingly urban world, the British Government's Department for International Development (DFID) has supported research on issues that can reduce poverty and improve living conditions for the urban poor in developing countries. This is particularly important as the MDGs concentrate on improving existing urban slums but do not address the equally important need to reduce the development of future slums. The challenge is therefore to develop a twin-track approach combining upgrading and options for new legal development, which meet the needs of the urban poor.

Among the many factors which influence access to new legal housing and the upgrading of existing informal settlements, regulatory frameworks establish the official requirements of planning standards, regulations and administrative procedures to which all officially sanctioned development must conform. Given that a significant proportion of urban development is presently unauthorized, it is important that the regulatory frameworks are appropriate to the needs and realities with which they have to contend.

This publication provides a practical method for reviewing and revising regulatory frameworks applicable to upgrading existing settlements and planning new housing development, that is affordable and appropriate to the needs of the poor. It is based on extensive international research undertaken by two teams made up of researchers, professionals and development practitioners, working on projects funded by DFID between 2001 and 2004.

One team, led by Theo Schilderman and Mike Majale of the Intermediate Technology Development Group (ITDG), focused on regulatory guidelines for urban upgrading and worked with partners in India (Society for the Development of Area-based Resources (SPARC), led by Sheela Patel), Kenya (Intermediate Technology Development Group–Eastern Africa (ITDG–EA), led by Rebecca

Kabura) and Sri Lanka (SEVANATHA–Urban Resource Centre (SEVANATHA–URC), led by K A Jayaratne).

The other team was led by Geoffrey Payne of Geoffrey Payne and Associates (GPA) and focused on regulatory guidelines for new affordable shelter with colleagues in Bolivia (Fabian Farfan of Universidad Mayor de San Simon, Bolivia), India (Uma Adusumilli and Dilip Shekdar of Maharashtra City and Industrial Development Corporation (CIDCO)), Lesotho (David Hall of Sechaba Consultants), South Africa (Lauren Royston of Development Works), Tanzania (Lusugga Kironde of the University College of Lands and Architectural Studies (UCLAS)) and Turkey (Ruşen Keleş of Ankara University).

A number of UK-based advisers also contributed, namely: Andrew Cotton and M Sohail (Water and Engineering Development Centre (WEDC), Loughborough University), Ruth McLeod (Homeless International) and Graham Tipple (Global Urban Research Unit, Newcastle University).

Geoffrey Payne and Michael Majale
June 2004

ACKNOWLEDGEMENTS

We would like to record our warm appreciation for the efforts of our partners in the case study countries and the UK for their creative contributions to the research projects on which this manual is based. Each has contributed ideas as well as information and responded patiently to repeated requests for more. The case study reports containing the substance of each team's efforts are contained on the CD-Rom. This has been edited by Evelyn Tehrani, to whom we also owe a special debt for her contribution in helping to edit the manual itself. Ripin Kalra contributed substantially to making both the document and CD-Rom visually attractive, while Edward MacDermott developed and formatted the latter. Rob West and Frances MacDermott at Earthscan pulled out all the stops to process editing and production. We would also like to thank all those colleagues who have been, and continue to be, involved in promoting more responsive and appropriate pro-poor regulatory frameworks for urban housing.

The strong support received throughout the projects from DFID is much appreciated. The views expressed in the following pages, however, are not necessarily those of DFID.

Geoffrey Payne and Michael Majale
June 2004

LIST OF ACRONYMS AND ABBREVIATIONS

CAP	community action planning
CBO	community-based organization
CDS	city development strategy
CIDCO	Maharashtra City and Industrial Development Corporation (India)
CLIFF	Community-Led Infrastructure Finance Facility
CSD	Commission on Sustainable Development
CZMP	Coastal Zone Management Plan (India)
DFID	Department for International Development, UK
GDP	gross domestic product
GOM	Government of Maharashtra (India)
GPA	Geoffrey Payne and Associates
Habitat II	United Nations Conference on Human Settlements, Istanbul, June 1996
HBE	home-based enterprise
ITDG	Intermediate Technology Development Group
ITDG–EA	Intermediate Technology Development Group – Eastern Africa (Kenya)
m	metre
MDG	Millennium Development Goal
MM	Mahila Milan
NGO	non-governmental organization
NSDF	National Federation of Slum Dwellers (India)
PIPs	policies, institutions and processes
SDI	Slum/Shack Dwellers International
SEVANATHA-URC	SEVANATHA-Urban Resource Centre (Kenya)
SL	sustainable livelihoods
SPARC	Society for the Development of Area-based Resources (India)
UCLAS	University College of Lands and Architectural Studies (Tanzania)
UDA	Urban Development Authority (Sri Lanka)
ULA	urban local authority (Sri Lanka)
UN	United Nations
UNCED	United Nations Conference on Environment and Development, Rio de Janeiro, Brazil, 1992 (known as the Earth Summit)
UNCHS (Habitat)	United Nations Centre for Human Settlements (Habitat) (now UN-HABITAT)

UN-HABITAT	United Nations Human Settlements Programme (*formerly* UNCHS (Habitat))
WEDC	Water and Engineering Development Centre (Loughborough University)
WSSD	World Summit on Sustainable Development, Johannesburg, South Africa, 2002

INTRODUCTION

WHAT THIS MANUAL IS ABOUT

This manual provides a conceptual and practical tool for those involved in reviewing and revising regulatory frameworks concerned with housing and urban development in developing countries. It addresses the upgrading of existing informal settlements and options for improving access to legal and affordable new housing.

The focus of the manual is on planning regulations, standards and administrative procedures involved in managing urban development, the upgrading of existing settlements and the development of new housing affordable to the poor. At present, the rules by which government agencies seek to manage and control urban development and housing – regulatory frameworks – have been largely ineffective, and countless households are living in various types of slums and unauthorized settlements. *The Urban Housing Manual* is intended to help all those involved in formulating, implementing or seeking to change regulatory frameworks so that existing slums can be upgraded and the need for new ones reduced through access to more affordable new housing.

The Urban Housing Manual is not intended to mean reducing standards so much as enabling more people, especially the poor, to be able to conform to regulatory frameworks which are appropriate to local conditions. As with a game, rules are intended to establish clear guidelines as to what people can and cannot do. Rules can provide an infinite variety of outcomes: two games of chess, cricket or soccer will never be the same. However, to be enforceable, rules need to command local acceptance and legitimacy. This manual identifies ways in which such regulatory frameworks can be made more meaningful and accessible, and so stimulate national and local economies and ensure that all sections of society, especially the poor and other vulnerable groups, participate in and benefit from processes of urbanization. It builds on previous work addressing building regulations and standards (eg Yahya et al, 2001) and on infrastructure provision and urban upgrading (eg Tayler and Cotton,

1993; Cotton and Tayler, 2000; Davidson and Payne, 2000). It also includes an application of the DFID sustainable livelihoods framework as presented in Ashley and Carney (1999).

WHO IT IS FOR

The manual is intended for policy-makers and urban administrators, professionals, development practitioners, staff in training institutions and international agencies, students and civic society groups engaged in urban development. Inevitably, such a diverse readership will have many perspectives, priorities and interests. However, it is assumed that these groups all have one thing in common: a desire to improve the urban areas where they live and work in ways which benefit all social groups, not just an affluent minority.

WHY IT WAS PRODUCED

The research projects on which this manual is based found that regulatory frameworks are:

- extremely influential in determining options for upgrading existing settlements and developing new officially sanctioned areas;
- often grossly inappropriate to the needs and resources available to governments, developers and residents, and actually contribute substantially to the widespread increase of unauthorized urban development;
- generally unknown to residents, many developers, professionals and sometimes even the officials responsible for implementing them; and
- a major constraint to the improvement of poor people's livelihoods and housing conditions in developing country cities and towns.

Rather than just publish reports confirming these findings, it was considered that a more useful outcome of the research would be to produce a manual to assist professionals and others working on urban development to identify the nature and extent to which planning regulations, standards and administrative procedures are appropriate, and how they might be made more appropriate to the needs of the poor while still protecting the public interest.

The manual seeks to address these issues by presenting a range of short notes covering definitions, concepts, methods of analysing existing regulatory frameworks and examples drawn from the case study countries. For readers interested in further information on the research or related sources of information, and those wishing to apply the methods to other contexts, a CD-Rom is provided.

The two teams carried out their research independently, although they were in frequent contact. The ITDG team focused on regulatory guidelines for upgrading existing informal settlements and adopted the sustainable livelihoods (SL) approach, while the GPA team addressed regulatory frameworks in terms of how they could improve access to new legal housing for the urban poor, and designed a framework for undertaking regulatory audits. The different approaches followed by the two teams have been incorporated into a single volume. The manual, together with the CD-Rom, is the outcome of this collective endeavour.

People living in urban areas all over the world are affected by regulatory frameworks in trying to access legal shelter and basic services.

HOW IT IS STRUCTURED

The manual is organized into seven parts. Following this short Introduction, Section 1 puts the issues of regulatory frameworks into their broad political, institutional, legal, economic and social contexts. As the roles of governments change due to globalization, economic and political forces, financial, institutional and technical constraints and ever-increasing demand, so the role of regulatory frameworks needs to be reviewed and options for improvement identified.

In Section 2, the main elements of regulatory frameworks are discussed and the roles of central, provincial and local governments, together with civil society groups, are explored. Key principles, essential if pro-poor regulatory frameworks are to be established and maintained in response to changing conditions, are also discussed.

Section 3 focuses on key issues which highlight the impacts that regulatory frameworks can have on the lives of the urban poor. This recognizes that there are different perceptions of planning regulations, standards and administrative procedures according to the perspective of the stakeholder. Thus, professionals educated to regard themselves as upholding decent standards and correct procedures, as enshrined in official statutes, will understandably regard any breach as unlawful and a threat to their professional integrity. Private developers, on the other hand, may regard complex administrative procedures as sources of delay and a means of extracting money from them by local bureaucrats. They have to pass these costs on to households buying into their developments in order to stay in business. Of course, this limits the degree to which they can serve the needs of those at the lower end of the market. Finally, households themselves are faced with a mass of official forms and offices which have to be visited in order to obtain official permissions and meet standards which impose costs that many cannot afford. In many cases, information is written in a language local people may not speak, or in a form which cannot be understood by anyone without professional training. In other cases, information is simply not available even in the municipal offices responsible for implementing regulatory guidelines. While such a brief summary may be a caricature of the reality, it demonstrates the different perspectives that clearly influence discussion concerning regulatory frameworks and also influence options for introducing change.

Section 4 presents two useful methodologies for reviewing regulatory frameworks: the SL approach and the regulatory audit. These two approaches reveal different characteristics of regulatory frameworks and the ways they impact on the livelihoods of the poor, upgrading interventions and new housing development. They can be used either individually or simultaneously to provide a more complete picture of existing regulatory frameworks and what, if anything, must be changed to make them more appropriate to local conditions. A discussion of important issues that must be kept in mind when choosing methods for reviewing existing regulatory frameworks can be found on the accompanying CD-Rom, which also contains more detailed descriptions, guidelines and advice for employing specific methods.

Section 5 reviews the key issues involved in effecting change and the principles that must be upheld in order to bring about pro-poor change. This assumes that, in many cases, pressure for change is more likely to come from those who feel unable to conform to existing regulatory frameworks than those responsible for enforcing them. Thus, private-sector developers working at the lower end of the market and particularly civil society groups such as non-governmental organizations (NGOs) and community-based organizations (CBOs) may find this section of particular use. It will also help public-sector officials to appreciate the reasons why changes may be needed and suggest ways in which they can be persuaded to support change.

This is not to suggest that fundamental changes are always needed to regulatory frameworks. In many cases, a small reduction in a planning standard, a minor relaxation of a restrictive regulation or a simplification of an administrative procedure can be enough to stimulate confidence in improving existing settlements or reducing costs for new developments. Given the changing macro-economic pressures operating in land and housing markets globally, together with changing patterns of housing need, it is inevitable that revisions will need to be made to regulatory frameworks on a regular basis, rather than once in a lifetime.

Key considerations in any effective regulatory framework for urban development will be the ways in which it defines and seeks to protect the public interest. This will be interpreted differently by different stakeholders in any one place and by the same stakeholder groups in different places and at different times. Possibly, all cases

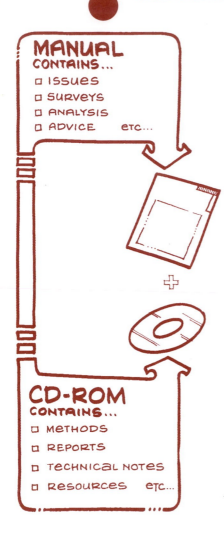

MANUAL
CONTAINS...

☐ ISSUES

☐ SURVEYS

☐ ANALYSIS

☐ ADVICE   ETC...

CD-ROM
CONTAINS...

☐ METHODS

☐ REPORTS

☐ TECHNICAL NOTES

☐ RESOURCES   ETC...

will be based on protecting public health and safety, although other measures may be presented as intended to achieve this when, in reality, the motivation may be very different.

Finally, Section 6 offers some concluding suggestions for further action.

To supplement the manual, the enclosed CD-Rom contains full details of the country case studies on which the manual is based, together with papers on specific aspects such as infrastructure, land tenure and property rights, housing, finance and home-based economic activities. Useful tools and exercises presented in the manual are also accessible on the CD-Rom, where they can be used interactively.

1 REGULATION AND REALITY

THE PROCESS OF URBAN GROWTH

Is urban growth in developing countries inevitable? Can it, or should it, be stopped, reduced or controlled, possibly by encouraging rural development programmes?

These questions have been asked of professionals, governments, researchers/academics and international agencies ever since developing countries began to experience a mass movement from rural to urban areas in the latter part of the last century.

Certainly, the scale of urbanization currently underway in developing countries is without parallel in human history. As United Nations (UN) statistics confirm (UN-Habitat, 2003a, p5), the world's population has increased from 2.5 billion in 1950 to 6 billion

The main challenge facing governments, the international community and civil society organizations involved in urban development and housing is to upgrade existing informal settlements and improve access to legal and affordable new housing

	Estimated and projected populations (millions)		
	1990	*2000*	*2015*
Abidjan, Côte d'Ivoire	2.19	3.79	6.08
Accra, Ghana	1.38	1.87	2.89
Ahmedabad, India	3.25	4.43	6.61
Cairo, Egypt	8.29	9.46	11.53
Dar es Salaam, Tanzania	1.31	2.11	4.08
Dhaka, Bangladesh	6.62	12.52	22.77
Jakarta, Indonesia	7.65	11.02	17.27
Johannesburg, South Africa	2.08	2.95	3.81
Lagos, Nigeria	4.77	8.67	15.97
Lima, Peru	5.82	7.44	9.39
Mexico City	15.31	18.06	20.43
São Paulo, Brazil	15.10	17.96	21.23

TABLE 1.1
Examples of urban growth rates in developing countries

Source: UN-Habitat, 2003a, Table C1

in 2002, of which 60 per cent has been in the urban areas of developing countries. As if this did not in itself present a massive challenge to governments, civil society and the international community, the global urban population is set to increase by more than 2 billion within 30 years, while rural populations remain virtually static or, in some cases, begin to decline. The projected increase in population globally represents an annual increase of about 70 million people, all of whom will need land, housing, services and, most importantly, work, primarily in urban areas.

These global figures are matched by evidence from individual countries (see Table 1.1). For example, the populations of some cities are increasing at more than 7 per cent per year, which suggests their populations will double within a decade. Many others will see substantial numerical increases, even with lower percentage growth rates.

Of course, it is always dangerous to assume that the future will be simply an extension of the past, and many large cities have, in fact, grown at less than the forecast rates. Conversely, many smaller secondary towns are growing at faster rates than the major cities. While variations are common, it is nonetheless a fact that urban growth has been accelerating for the last few decades and shows no sign of stopping in the foreseeable future. Attempts to stop or control urban growth have proved expensive and ineffective, and are possibly incompatible with the principle of freedom of movement enshrined in most democratic constitutions.

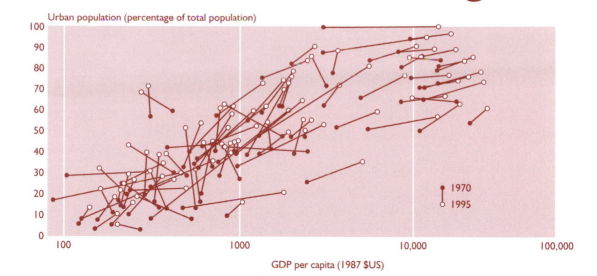

Urban population (percentage of total population)

GDP per capita (1987 $US)

● 1970
○ 1995

FIGURE 1.1
**Urbanization is
closely related to
economic growth**

Source: World Bank,
*World Development
Indicators,* 1999, p126

It is also important to remember that a high proportion of urban population growth is due to the natural increase of the existing population rather than rural–urban migration. Expanding rural development programmes would not, therefore, significantly reduce urban population growth rates. In addition, urban areas contribute a significant proportion of central government resources, including those for rural development, so healthy, dynamic urban areas are essential for national and regional development. Moreover, international data (eg UNCHS, 1996, p28; World Bank, 1999, p126) show a direct correlation between levels of urbanization and economic development, so that urban growth can broadly be associated with economic progress rather than decline (see Figure 1.1). The challenge is therefore how to manage the process of urban growth, rather than how to prevent or reduce it.

THE URBANIZATION OF POVERTY

One result of urban growth is the urbanization of poverty. A significant and increasing proportion of the growing urban populations are living on low incomes. For example, more than three-quarters of the poor in Latin America already live in cities, and many poverty-related problems – such as a lack of secure housing, or access to water and sanitation – tend to be more prevalent in urban than rural areas (UN-Habitat, 2001, p15). Current indicators, such as per capita incomes of less than a dollar a day, do not take into account the increased costs of living in urban areas and the difficulty of living outside the cash economy. While urban incomes, even for rural–urban migrants, are often substantially higher than those in rural areas, these higher living costs force the poor into spending a high proportion of their incomes on basic human needs, including food, water and housing. It has been estimated that nearly 1 billion urban residents in developing countries are poor, and their numbers are increasing more rapidly than in rural areas.

While the statistics are daunting, they do not convey the human dimension of the challenge. Every morning, nearly 1 billion people (UN-Habitat, 2003a, p14) wake up in insecure, substandard homes facing an uncertain day, let alone a future. Children are born into lives where clean water and healthy diets are unknown, and attending school is a dream beyond the reach of many. Economic deprivation puts family life under pressure and drugs, drink or gambling offer tempting, if temporary, escape routes for some. The vast majority, however, battle on from day to day, sacrificing their own lives in the hope of something better for their children.

Similar problems faced the urban poor in 19th-century Britain, when cholera epidemics and other diseases wiped out whole swathes of the urban populations before public health legislation ensured access to basic services and improved the environment. Even then, however, it took several decades before institutional capability developed sufficiently to raise standards that could be called adequate, despite Britain's economic pre-eminence and the relatively small numbers of people involved. Given the far larger numbers and the limited human, technical and financial resources available to governments in developing countries, it is hardly surprising that they have been overwhelmed and are struggling to resolve their problems.

THE GROWTH OF SLUMS AND INFORMAL SETTLEMENTS

Rapid urbanization and urban growth have placed immense pressure on the resources of national and local governments. Few have been able to meet the increasing need for planned and affordable land, housing and services either through direct provision or incentives to the private sector. The result is that millions of people around the world have found their own solution in various types of slums and

Box 1.1 What is a slum?

A slum is a contiguous settlement where the inhabitants are characterized as having inadequate housing and basic services. A slum is often not recognized and addressed by the public authorities as an integral or equal part of the city.

Target 11 of the Millennium Development Goals (MDGs) describes typical slums in developing countries as 'unplanned informal settlements where access to services is minimal to non-existent and where overcrowding is the norm. Slum conditions result in placing residents at a higher risk of disease, mortality and misfortune'.

A review of different slum definitions by UN-Habitat revealed the following attributes of slums:

- Lack of basic services.
- Substandard housing or illegal and inadequate building structures.
- Overcrowding and high density.
- Unhealthy living conditions and hazardous locations.
- Insecure tenure; irregular or informal settlements.
- Poverty and social exclusion.

Source: UN-Habitat, 2003a, p10

unauthorized or informal settlements (see Box 1.1). Ironically, these often reflect the socio-economic and cultural needs of low-income communities more than the official forms of development favoured by professionals and government agencies.

According to UN estimates there are at present 924 million people living in such settlements, which are also the most conspicuous manifestations of the urbanization of poverty (UN-Habitat, 2003a, p2). The number is expected to increase to 2 billion (2000 million) by 2030 unless major changes are made to the present policies and practices of urban management. This requires a dramatic increase in efforts to improve living conditions in existing slums and informal settlements, and to reduce the existing numbers down to modest levels. It also requires an acceptance that unless access to legal shelter is made more affordable and accessible to the majority of the urban poor, the growth of such unauthorized settlements will continue unabated. This is obviously not good news for the poor who have to endure substandard and, in some cases, subhuman living conditions on the margins of urban society. However, neither is it in the interests of the more fortunate affluent minority, since they will also be affected directly or indirectly by the health risks and other consequences of social alienation to which the poor are exposed. The main challenge facing governments, the international community and civil society organizations involved in urban development and housing is therefore to develop a twin-track approach that aims to upgrade existing informal settlements and improve access to legal and affordable new housing.

While the global statistics are dramatic, they do not necessarily translate into meaningful numbers for those trying to solve problems in a particular country or city. The problem is compounded by national variations in measuring slums. Yet, a random selection of cities shows that the problem is real for planners. For example, in Ahmedabad, India, the slum population has increased from 17.1 per cent in 1971, to 21.4 per cent in 1982 and to about 40 per cent in 1991. This also has to be seen in the context of an increasing total. Similarly, in Kolkata, India, 1.5 million people live in registered and unregistered slums, while in Karachi, Pakistan, estimates suggest an increase of 50 per cent between 1998 and 2000, from 3.4 to 5 million people. In São Paulo, Brazil, more than 80 per cent of the population growth during the 1980s was absorbed by the *favelas*, while in Nairobi, Kenya, about 60 per cent of the population live in informal settlements. Sub-Saharan Africa is the region with the highest proportion of urban residents in slums, at 71.9 per cent (UN-Habitat, 2003a).

Estimating the scale and nature of existing unauthorized or substandard urban development poses problems of definition as well as of measurement. Each country has its own definition of what constitutes slums or substandard housing, and the accuracy of data varies considerably.

INTERNATIONAL RESPONSES TO URBAN POVERTY, SLUMS AND INFORMAL SETTLEMENTS

The international community and national governments have agreed a range of policy measures in recent years to address the problems of urban poverty and access to affordable, adequate and appropriate housing. These include the following:

The Habitat Agenda

This was adopted by 171 governments at the United Nations Conference on Human Settlements (Habitat II), Istanbul in June

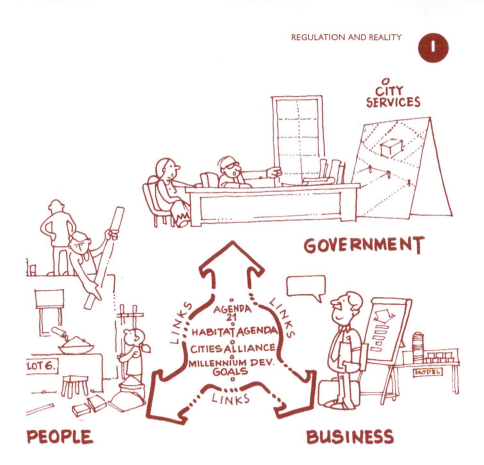

1996. It provides a practical roadmap to an urbanizing world, setting out approaches and strategies towards the achievement of two main objectives: ensuring adequate shelter for all and the sustainable development of the world's urban areas. The key commitments of the Agenda to achieving these goals include the following:

- Enablement and participation.
- Gender equality.
- Financing shelter and human settlements.
- International cooperation.
- Assessment and monitoring of progress.

The Habitat Agenda represents a fundamental reorientation of policy in the management of human settlements. In particular, the concept of 'enablement' recognizes that governments are not able to meet housing needs through direct action or state provision, and that the diversity and scale of such needs requires the participation of the private sector and local communities. In this new environment, the role of the state is to enable other stakeholders to take the lead in

The international community and national governments have agreed a range of policy measures in recent years to address the problem of urban poverty and access to affordable, adequate and appropriate housing

providing land and housing, with the state regulating the market and targeting actions to help the poor and other vulnerable groups. Regulatory frameworks thus have a pivotal role in determining the success of the Habitat Agenda.

In June 2001, five years after Habitat II, the UN General Assembly held a special session to review and appraise implementation of the Habitat Agenda worldwide.[1]

Agenda 21: promoting sustainable human settlement development

Agenda 21 was adopted at the United Nations Conference on Environment and Development (UNCED or 'Earth Summit') held in Rio de Janeiro, Brazil, in 1992. It is a comprehensive plan of action to be taken globally, nationally and locally by UN agencies, governments and major groups in every area in which humans impact on the environment. A major theme of Agenda 21 is the need to eradicate poverty by giving poor people more access to the resources they need for sustainable living.

The Agenda covers three main areas, each with a number of goals for which programme areas, objectives, and actions and means of implementation are outlined:

1   Social and economic dimensions, including international cooperation to combat poverty, improve health and integrate environmental management in decision-making.
2   The conservation and management of resources for development, including the management of land resources, combating deforestation and desertification, and protecting freshwater resources.
3   Strengthening the role of major groups, especially women, young people, NGOs, local authorities and the private sector.

The Commission on Sustainable Development (CSD) was also created in December 1992 to ensure effective follow-up to UNCED, and to monitor and report on the implementation of the agreements at the local, national, regional and international levels. It was agreed that a five-year review of Earth Summit progress would be made in 1997 by the UN General Assembly. The CSD stated that while extensive efforts had been made by governments, international organizations and local grass-roots groups to implement the

Agenda, there is still a long way to go. The impact of globalization on developing countries has been uneven and only a few countries have been able to benefit. Many other countries, especially in Africa, have seen economic conditions worsen and public services deteriorate, as a result of which they face high levels of poverty, low levels of social development and inadequate infrastructures. These countries still require international assistance in their efforts to achieve sustainable development.

The full implementation of Agenda 21 and the commitments of the Rio Principles were reaffirmed at the World Summit on Sustainable Development (WSSD) held in South Africa in 2002.[2]

Cities Alliance[3]

In 1999, the World Bank and UN-Habitat founded Cities Alliance to address the above issues. The Alliance consists of four constituencies:

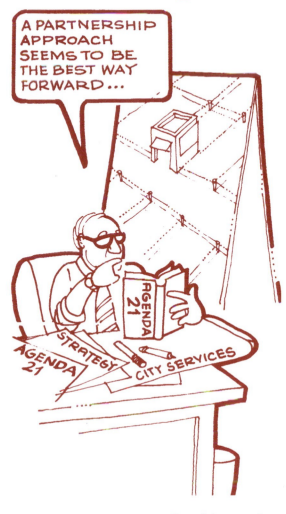

1   The urban poor themselves.
2   Local authorities and their associations.
3   National governments.
4   Multilateral and bilateral agencies.

The objective of Cities Alliance is to realize the vision of 'cities without slums' through action plans in two key areas (UN-Habitat, 2003a, p140):

One of the aims of international policy agreements is to strengthen the role and partnerships between major groups such as women, young people, NGOs, local authorities and the private sector in the delivery of sustainable urban development

1   City development strategies (CDSs) by which local stakeholders define their vision for their city, analyse its economic prospects and establish clear priorities for actions and investments.
2   City-wide and nation-wide slum upgrading to improve the living conditions of at least 100 million slum dwellers by 2020.

The Millennium Development Goals (MDGs)[4]

The MDGs were agreed at the UN in 2000 and seek to integrate the principles of sustainable development into country policies and programmes, and set global targets for different sectors to be achieved by specified dates. While many would go a long way to reducing global poverty and improving the quality of life for the world's poor, this does not apply in the case of urban development, for which there are two key targets. The most significant is Goal 7, in which Target 10 seeks to halve by 2015 the proportion of people without sustainable access to safe drinking water and basic sanitation, and Target 11 seeks to have achieved by 2020 a significant improvement in the lives of at least 100 million slum dwellers. However, this target falls well short of the 924 million people presently estimated to live in slums and squatter settlements. It also does nothing to reduce the growth of future slums and informal settlements, which are projected to increase to 2 billion people by 2030. In reality, the need is for a far more ambitious programme – a twin-track approach that aims to upgrade existing informal settlements and improve access to legal and affordable new housing (Payne, 2003).

NATIONAL ISSUES IN REGULATORY FRAMEWORKS

International agreements are not the only influences on government policies and practices concerning urban development. Globalization in particular has generated pressures on governments to deregulate and privatize whole swathes of economic life, and to reduce direct state intervention in social and welfare programmes, including the provision of housing, public services and communal facilities. Cities are being forced to compete internationally for external investment, and vast capital sums are placed wherever policies and regulatory frameworks offer the greatest returns and lowest risks. This does not make it easier to protect the public from lower standards, but does justify a reassessment of existing norms.

The role of the state in development is changing fundamentally as market forces penetrate all aspects of economic and even social life. Direct control of urban land and housing markets is no longer possible. However, it is possible to guide the processes of growth and change, and to create an enabling environment as embodied in the Habitat Agenda. In fact, public-sector influence over such markets may be greater through regulatory mechanisms than through conventional attempts to influence such markets through subsidies or direct provision.

Now that the essential components of urban and housing policies are in place, increasing attention should be paid to addressing and removing constraints on the effective implementation of such policies. Regulatory frameworks are likely candidates for such attention. It will also be important to adapt regulatory frameworks from one area to another, especially if climatic or ground conditions vary from one part of a country to another (see Box 1.2).

CITY-LEVEL ISSUES IN REGULATORY FRAMEWORKS

As urban areas grow and the need for more low-income households to obtain housing, services and work increases, so the need increases for policies and regulatory frameworks to facilitate upgrading and new planned development. This requires the relevant authorities to continually review the relationship between needs and costs when seeking to promote economic development and protect the environment.

This issue can be illustrated by comparing land budgets and estimates of housing needs for a city over a period of ten years. Of course, there are many external factors which will influence the area of land required. These include national and regional economic investment, development and growth patterns; human or environmental disasters within the hinterland which could lead to mass migration; the attraction of alternative regional centres; and the physical availability of land.

Box 1.2 Localized norms

There are no universal norms which can be adopted to meet varied conditions. Each society will determine its own definitions of what is acceptable based on cultural, climatic, social and economic considerations. Even within countries, there will sometimes be a need for variations. For example, in Papua New Guinea settlements on the coast need to encourage ventilation and protect residents from heat and humidity, whereas just 30km inland, settlements at 3500m (12,000 feet) above sea level need to maximize insulation and protection from frost. National regulations cannot easily apply to both cases.

While these external factors will be significant and are difficult to predict, uncertainty can be reduced considerably by estimating demand for land based on factors that are easier to predict. For example, if the existing urban population is increasing by 7 per cent per year, it will double in approximately ten years.[5] While a large proportion of the increased population can be expected to find housing within the existing urban area, many households will need to be accommodated on newly urbanized land. If existing planning standards such as density levels and minimum plot sizes are applied, this will indicate the additional land area required for a given population over a specified period. Where these standards show that the land required is more than is available, or the costs of servicing or providing it with a viable transportation system are too high, it may be advisable to revise such standards.

Similarly, future housing needs can be assessed by estimating the following:

*   The rate and scale of new household formation.
*   The replacement of existing units that will have fully depreciated during the plan period.
*   The replacement of deficient units whose upgrading is not economically feasible.
*   The number of units required to relieve overcrowding levels present at the start of the plan period.
*   The upgrading of deficient units existing at the start of the plan period, where this is economically feasible.

It should be remembered that estimates of housing deficit based on these or any other considerations need to be treated with great caution, since the criteria by which they are defined are partly subjective. Such estimates are useful in indicating the scale of housing needed to accommodate future population growth, and therefore the amount of land and services needed. Where the cost of officially approved housing exceeds the amount that different sections of the population are able to afford, ways will need to be found of reducing entry costs.

The recognition of incremental development processes by which households obtain or improve a basic unit that they can expand and improve over time is a sensible approach which is widely adopted by the poor themselves. Revising or relaxing planning regulations to

facilitate upgrading and more affordable new housing is another key option. Methods of carrying out such studies can be found on the accompanying CD-Rom. For the purposes of this manual, the important point is that the ability to provide both land and housing in a planned manner will be significantly influenced by the regulatory framework.

If the responsibility for formulating and revising regulatory frameworks is concentrated at national or provincial levels of government, the scope for local authorities to effect change will be restricted. Where local government is only responsible for enforcement, this may lead to failure if elements of the regulatory framework are not appropriate to local conditions or are too demanding of scarce local resources. This problem will be exacerbated if there are different requirements for the upgrading of existing low-income settlements and the planning of new ones. (See Section 2, 'Comparing new developments with upgrading', p30, for a full discussion of regulatory frameworks for upgrading and for new development.)

It will be important to identify those groups seeking to maintain existing regulatory frameworks and those seeking to effect change.

The responsibilities for formulating and enforcing legislation have to be shared carefully between the various tiers of government. In this way contradictions can be avoided, the elements of regulatory frameworks will be more appropriate to local conditions and the ability of people to effect change will not be compromised

SETTLEMENT-LEVEL ISSUES IN REGULATORY FRAMEWORKS

It is perhaps at the settlement level that the impact of regulatory frameworks on urban development in developing countries is manifested most conspicuously. The urban poor majority live and work in polluted environments in informal settlements that have developed without regulatory control, and where their health and safety is at risk.

People find their own solutions by investing what they can over a period of time. While the initial development may be more modest than formal schemes, this can provide a platform for substantial future development

A key issue at settlement level is thus the extent to which regulatory frameworks reflect the needs, priorities and affordability of local communities. One way of assessing this is to compare the planning standards, regulations and procedures followed in the development of officially sanctioned developments and those followed in typical examples of unauthorized developments (see regulatory matrix tool on the accompanying CD-Rom). In cases where the informal settlements have been developed with the active participation or control of the residents themselves, it can reasonably be assumed that they reflect cultural and social priorities in the allocation of land and public space. Where these aspects are at significant variance with official requirements, it suggests that official norms need to be revised or at least relaxed.

A related issue is how far the use of discretion is permitted. For example, in cases where land uses do not conform to a specific regulation, standard or procedure, is there provision for relaxation or retrospective approval where the degree of non-conformity is relatively minor and there is no local objection? Does this help communities or is it a means of abuse by local officials?[6]

KEY QUESTIONS

- What has been the urban population growth rate in your country since 1990?

- How do growth rates vary from city to city and what are the reasons for this?

- What has been the annual gross domestic product (GDP) growth rate in your country since 1990?

- What is the projected population increase of your city?

- What are the key factors driving the growth of your city and how are these likely to change in time? (for example, in Lesotho the rapid growth of garment factories is a key factor, but this is unlikely to continue indefinitely).

- Are local planning policies based on a realistic assessment of population growth rates?

- How is poverty defined in your country/city?

- What proportion of the urban population is defined as poor?

- How rapidly is the proportion of poor households increasing?

- How are slums and informal settlements defined in your country or city? Is a distinction made between slums, squatter areas, unplanned areas and informal settlements?

- Are slums or informal settlements exclusively occupied by the poor, or also by higher-income groups?

- What interest groups benefit from the development of slums?

- What are the biggest risks posed by slum development that regulation should address?

- What are the biggest constraints preventing slum dwellers from accessing legal land?

2 REGULATION AND REGULATORY FRAMEWORKS

Regulatory frameworks should be used as tools to incorporate urban realities and the public interest into the vision of the planner

REGULATION IN A GLOBAL ENVIRONMENT

Globalization has intensified pressure on all countries to compete with each other to attract inward investment. International corporations scour the world seeking opportunities to invest in sectors and countries which yield the highest possible return at the lowest possible risk. In this environment, organizations such as the World Trade Organization and International Monetary Fund put pressure on borrowers to reduce regulatory constraints to such investment. The same strategy is applied to stimulating domestic investment in increasing economic productivity and reducing poverty.

The merits or otherwise of this approach to development are the subject of a large and rapidly increasing literature. This is not the place to review that. However, it does set the context for any discussion of regulatory frameworks for urban development in that it raises the question of the objectives of regulatory frameworks for urban development and housing.[1] Are they primarily intended to establish minimum standards, regulations and procedures for those unable to afford market-determined prices for obtaining assets such as land, housing and services? Are they intended primarily to reduce constraints on investors and developers? Are they intended to ensure planned development in the allocation and development of land which meets cultural and social needs?

The answer to all these questions is essentially that the regulatory framework for new urban development and upgrading needs to accommodate all these aspects. Failure to attract investment will not create the wealth needed to meet poverty reduction targets. Similarly, standards that do not permit a quality of life sufficient to ensure a healthy social life are unlikely to be sustainable. The essential characteristic of an effective regulatory framework is therefore one which strikes a balance between these often conflicting requirements.

THE IMPACT OF REGULATORY FRAMEWORKS

Regulatory frameworks have a significant bearing on urban development in general, and, in particular, on planning, zoning, land use and plot development, space standards and infrastructure services. Under conditions of globalization, a regulatory framework is also one of the few instruments available to governments to influence urban land and housing markets, and the investment decisions of private-sector developers. Regulatory frameworks therefore have significant implications for the physical, economic, social and technological environments of poor communities, and impact directly or indirectly on their livelihoods.

Ironically, governments do not seem to have realized the potential influence which regulatory frameworks have on urban land and housing markets, and the ability of the poor to access legal housing. This is perhaps due in part to the fact that planning regulations, standards and administrative procedures were formulated at a time when urban populations were relatively small and affluent, and growth rates were modest. Now that cities are larger, populations are predominantly poor and growth rates are high, it is imperative that the relationship between standards, regulations and procedures be related more clearly to the costs and resources available to meet them. This makes it urgent to review regulatory frameworks to assess where changes are necessary to reflect current realities.

A key consideration in reviewing and revising regulatory frameworks is the need to identify the main features which represent the public interest in urban development. These will usually relate to issues of public health, environmental protection and social welfare. Ideally, they should be based on the minimum initial criteria for achieving these objectives rather than ideal long-term targets. These issues are discussed in more detail later in this section (see 'Why regulate? The pros and cons of regulation', p35). By concentrating on essentials it will be easier for government to inform other stakeholders of what is expected of them and to enforce agreed norms.

DEFINITIONS

'Regulation' can be conceived of as a rule or order of conduct prescribed by an authority, either requiring or prohibiting certain behaviour for various purposes such as health, safety or environmental objectives. It can also be regarded as a process or activity in which an authority requires or proscribes[2] certain activities or behaviour on the part of individuals, communities, organizations or institutions through a continuing administrative process, generally involving specially designated regulatory agencies.

Regulatory frameworks generally comprise legal and semi-legal instruments,[3] and may include policy documents, laws/legislation, bylaws, customary traditions, regulations (planning, building, financial, audit etc), standards (services and products) and procedures (procurement, design, public works, financial, audit etc) related to town planning, land development, building and public health.

Central and local governments establish regulatory frameworks to set the parameters for development in general, but more specifically for the city or municipal environment. While central governments are responsible for establishing the legal and policy framework, many local authorities are empowered to exercise delegated powers over urban development, although the situation varies considerably from one country to another. Since regulatory frameworks significantly influence the capacity of urban poor people to take a lead in their own development and achieve sustainable livelihoods, it is important that the right balance is struck between national and local needs and conditions.

In this manual, regulatory frameworks are considered to consist of three main elements:[4]

1   *Planning regulations*, which stipulate what development is permitted on urban land.
2   *Planning standards*, which stipulate the level or quality to which all officially acceptable land and housing development should conform.
3   *Administrative procedures*, which stipulate the official steps that all urban developments must follow to be officially acceptable.

Planning regulations generally comprise legal and semi-legal instruments and may include statutory rules, court rules, local rules, orders-in-council, proclamations, notices, guidelines, ministerial directions, codes of practice and so on. They have a bearing on planning, zoning, land use and plot development, space allocation and infrastructure services.

Regulations form a key element in regulatory frameworks. They are often complex and may be restrictive in seeking to prevent development which is considered unacceptable or contrary to social or environmental policy objectives. Some regulations may be clearly essential and enjoy widespread public support, such as preventing or controlling polluting industries in residential areas. However, other

Box 2.1 Plot sizes in Lesotho: the rural–urban divide

In Lesotho, new migrants arriving in the city come with expectations regarding land that are influenced by their rural backgrounds. The plot sizes in rural villages tend to be generous, allowing for privacy and small-scale farming or gardening. Land in rural areas is allocated without payment and the principle of equity is central to traditional land allocation practices, with new households asserting their rights to plots as large as those allocated to others. In addition to enjoying free land to build on, the Basotho population in rural areas have enjoyed the freedom to build as they want with no building permits required. When arriving in urban areas, rural migrants accept that they have to pay for land, but still expect plot sizes to be generous. As a result the city continues to spread with only limited densification taking place in the more established areas. One outcome of this is poor service delivery in the peri-urban areas.

Source: Hall, 2004 (see CD-Rom)

regulations, such as 'building setbacks' from the side or rear of residential plots, do not enable residents to fully develop their plots and may achieve no benefit for the wider community. The fact that they may be based on concern about fire hazards can be resolved by constructions that are fire resistant. To be effective and acceptable to the general public, it is essential that planning regulations are perceived as relevant to the local context and not unduly restrictive (see Box 2.1).

Planning standards are technical specifications to which all approved development must conform. They cover physical requirements for plot size, road widths, public open space and infrastructure provision. Regulations are usually based on official perceptions of what is considered a minimum level or quality. However, standards imply costs and such costs are not always considered when standards are being determined. A key consideration is therefore that no matter how relevant planning

To be effective and acceptable to the general public, it is essential that planning regulations are perceived as relevant to the local conditions and not unduly excessive

standards may be environmentally or socially, they can only be enforced if residents or governments are able to finance them. In addition to issues of cost, planning regulations often take no account of the effect of the development on the ability to use it to improve livelihoods, for instance, through subletting or home-based enterprises.

In practice, the distinction between regulations and standards may be difficult to establish. For example, a requirement that buildings should not exceed a specified proportion of plot area may be considered either a planning regulation or a standard. It is less important which category a component is located under; the important thing is to make sure it is listed and assessed. The regulatory audit matrix (see Table 4.3 on p92 and accompanying CD-Rom) gives one example of how regulations, standards and administrative procedures can be listed and assessed.

Administrative procedures are the way by which regulations and standards are enforced and monitored. These encompass all activities, from applying to register, develop or transfer land for housing, to changing land use, obtaining permission to build or upgrading existing settlements (see Box 2.2). Procedures may be listed in codes of practice, administrative orders, management instructions or other statutory instruments (see Box 2.3). Some may be established specifically for issues of urban management, while

Administrative procedures may require extensive visits to different government departments, and different application forms, permits, certificates or licences. All these take time and increase the official and unofficial costs of conforming to regulatory requirements

Box 2.2 Typical steps in making legal land available in Dar es Salaam, Tanzania

Step	Action	Typical duration
1	Identification of a suitable area	
2	Notification of property owners	6 months
3	Declaration of area as planning area	1 year
4	Valuation of existing interests	1 year
5	Effecting payment of compensation	1–2 years
6	Preparation of town planning scheme	1–2 years
7	Approval of town planning scheme, Urban Planning Committee	6 months
8	Approval of town planning scheme by the ministry	6 months
9	Land surveying	1–2 years
10	Approval of survey	1–9 years
11	Letters of offer (entry point into legality)	1–6 months
12	Acceptance	1 month
13	Issuing of certificate of title	1– many years

Source: Ministry of Lands, Dar es Salaam City Council, Dar es Salaam Municipalities

Thus seven or more years can elapse between the identification of an area for implementing a planning scheme to the time letters of offer are issued. Each of the steps shown above has its own internal sub-steps that are not shown here. Land surveying, for example, must go through 17 steps, which can take anything from a few months to several years (Silayo, 2002).

Source: Kironde, 2004 (see CD-Rom)

others may form an integral part of wider civil service practice. Reform of the former will therefore be easier than the latter. Some may be extensions of previous practices, while others may be stand-alone measures.

Taken together, procedures may require extensive visits to different government departments, and different official application forms and permits, certificates or licences. All these take time and increase the official and unofficial costs of conforming to regulatory requirements (see Box 2.4). A further consideration is that administrative procedures are often drafted in ways that only professionals can understand, making it almost impossible for the general public to understand what is expected of them. In some countries, even the officials responsible for implementing the regulatory framework are unaware of the specific details (see Box 2.5).

2

Box 2.3 Complexity of regulatory requirements in Kenya

A study of statutory regulatory requirements applicable to urban development in Mavoko municipality in Kenya revealed that a potential developer has to contend with over 22 Acts of Parliament that relate to urban development. This situation is further complicated by the fact that a number of these Acts may or may not have a direct bearing on the development in question. In addition, some are enforced at the discretion of a particular official. The range of legislation and regulatory requirements that may apply to a given development becomes more complex still when use is taken into consideration – for example, industrial health and safety requirements.

What makes the situation especially frustrating is not so much that relevant legislation is not consolidated in one document or authority, but that it is virtually impossible for a lay person to tell, or even be aware of, what legislation applies to their development. For instance, some relevant legislation is to be found in such unexpected places as the Security and Public Order Act and the Penal Code. In fact, officials responsible for enforcing an Act may be unaware of, or choose to disregard, the effect that a ruling in their jurisdiction may have on another. For example, it was found that a new development had been approved by the planning authorities, even though it was evident that the development would be ruled unfit for human settlement under the Public Health Act.

The net effect of this complexity and ambiguity is that developers tend to conform only to regulatory requirements that cannot be avoided, and deal with compliance with others in an ad hoc way should they need to. This not only defeats their purpose, but also exposes the developers to extortion. Moreover, the numerous legislative and regulatory regimes involve a multitude of steps and associated transaction costs which push up the cost of new developments.

Source: ITDG–EA, 2003 (see CD-Rom)

COMPARING NEW DEVELOPMENTS WITH UPGRADING

It should not be assumed that regulatory frameworks are identical for upgrading and new urban development (see Box 2.6). The high densities found in many unauthorized settlements may make it impractical to impose the standards required for new developments. For example, in the Kampung Improvement Programme in Indonesia, pathways are routinely just 2m wide and plot sizes may be smaller than $30m^2$, although in new developments the official minima are 3.5m and $54m^2$ respectively. To impose the standards for new development in inner city kampungs would require the relocation of a high proportion of existing residents.

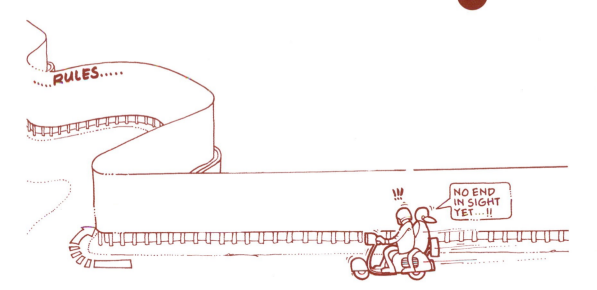

The main difference is that with upgrading there is usually some sort of negotiation with the community, so a compromise on standards is often agreed. Hence features such as plots of varying size and irregular shape are more likely to be accepted. The implementing agencies also often provide more assistance to households in upgrading projects: for example, the installation of services; the provision of type house designs and other technical assistance; the bulk purchase of building materials; loans and credit schemes; and sometimes training. In some cases, community management, including the routine maintenance of services, is encouraged, rather than this being done by the local authority or another outside operator. Communal services are likely to be more accepted, with individual water, toilet and sewerage facilities not needed for each plot. Earth roads, rather than asphalt or concrete, are more likely to be allowed (see Box 2.7). If an established community of squatters is resettled on new plots, the regulation of the settlement development is sometimes similar to that of an upgrading project, especially if they receive serviced plots or core housing units.

Administrative procedures are often incomprehensible and based on criteria which are difficult to follow

ORIGINS OF REGULATORY FRAMEWORKS

There are many differences between the processes of urbanization taking place in developing countries today and those that took place in Europe and North America in the 19th century. However, they have two aspects in common. One is that urban growth is irresistible

2

Box 2.4 Cost of conforming to regulations in Navi Mumbai new town

In Navi Mumbai, India, the land is in public ownership. As a result, some problematic procedures such as the verification of land titles, the granting of permission to convert land from agricultural to non-agricultural use, the measurement of land area, etc are not required. The costs associated with such procedures are also eliminated. Land is thus allotted to lower-income groups on a subsidized basis. The costs of land development for the low-income groups can be broadly divided into four categories: land costs (10 per cent), legal costs of obtaining permissions (17 per cent), unofficial costs of obtaining the permissions (5 per cent) and construction costs (68 per cent). The legal cost of obtaining permissions itself involves the costs of property registration (3 per cent), obtaining development permission (31 per cent), hiring architectural services (10 per cent) and obtaining utility connections (56 per cent).

When undeveloped plots are allocated to low-income groups, it generally takes up to six years before they are able to develop them. When a group allotment is made to heterogeneous households, the initial coming together and pooling of resources takes longer than the actual construction. When individual households develop plots, the construction takes much longer. This is due to their limited capacity to manage construction and the time required to complete construction in accordance with the household's needs and capabilities.

The purchase and development of a plot involves more than 25 steps before a household can start living in the house. But more than 15 of these steps will not be necessary if it is a fully built apartment unit. In the case of ready-built apartments, occupation of the houses may take anything between 1 and 24 months depending on whether the houses are marketed before or after construction.

Source: Adusumilli and Shekdar, 2004 (see CD-Rom)

and generally promotes economic growth and opportunity, albeit with severe problems of adjustment. Second, they share a similar regulatory framework of planning regulations, standards and administrative procedures by which the relevant authorities seek to manage urban growth and development. In fact, the regulatory framework of many countries was established during the last century by colonial regimes or imported as part of development assistance programmes.

A substantial proportion of legislation, institutional structures, administrative procedures and professional interests in developing countries continue to apply urban planning and development control processes based on British or other colonial approaches. For

Box 2.5 Complex land allocation procedures in Kenya

The process of securing tenure on public land in Kenya was found to be protracted and to involve an exceedingly large number of officials. Each step has to go through several officials who, knowing the value of land, are able to take unlawful advantage of applicants. The very groups that are intended to benefit from allocations of public land – the poor and business developers – are thus excluded as they are often unable to see the application through. On the other hand, the politically well-connected who manage to secure land hold it for speculative purposes, thereby inflating the value and constraining urban development. In practice, most of the public land in Kenya, including Mavoko municipality, is allocated through direct application. Mavoko Municipal Council consequently does not know who owns most of the land under its jurisdiction. Large tracts of land thus remain undeveloped, while the Council has to contend with a shortage of residential land as its planning mandate has been seriously compromised.

Source: ITDG–EA, 2003 (see CD-Rom)

example, in many ex-British colonies, the British Town and Country Planning Act of 1947 was adopted almost in its entirety, and even now versions of it remain on the statute books in several countries, including India, Kenya and Tanzania. It was, however, not designed to address the problems that faced the majority of local people then or today.

Regulatory frameworks for urban development as applied in most developing countries have thus failed to provide orderly and sustainable urban development. Imposing planning regulations, standards and administrative procedures designed for very different conditions on populations that are invariably too poor to conform to them has led to respect for the law and official institutions in general being undermined. Where a small proportion of the population fail to conform to official rules and regulations, it is reasonable to interpret this as a bad reflection on that particular group. When the majority of the population do not conform, it is equally reasonable to conclude that it is a bad reflection on the rules and regulations to which they are being expected to conform (see Box 2.8).

Reviews of regulatory frameworks pointing to the need for more appropriate and flexible planning regulations, standards and procedures have been conducted internationally for nearly 30 years. In Kenya, for example, a condition for funding for one of the World Bank's first urban housing projects was that a review be carried out of the existing planning and building regulations and standards.

Box 2.6 Differences between regulations for urban upgrading and new development in Mumbai, India

- In Mumbai there are several sets of regulations: regulations for general developments, regulations for low-income housing, regulations governing slum upgrading, regulations for the redevelopment of old structures etc. Standards and regulations for low-income housing tend to be lower in relation to densities (reflected by high densities), open spaces (usually small in area), minimum room size (usually smaller rooms) etc. But standards and regulations governing the redevelopment of slums and other old housing are worked out on an entirely different basis. The aim in these cases is to make redevelopment for the original dwellers free of cost by increasing the development potential of the land. Additional development, which can be sold in the open market to offset the cost of typical sized units for the original dwellers, is thus permissible. This market-based approach, however, can only work under favourable market conditions.
- In Navi Mumbai, the standards and regulations for low-income housing developed by public housing agencies are different from those applicable to general development. Slum redevelopment schemes along these lines are now proposed.

Standards were lowered for different reasons in the above situations. In the case of new developments for low-income groups by public agencies, it was to make housing units affordable to the households and to reduce the subsidy for public housing authorities. In the case of the rehabilitation of units under the slum redevelopment scheme in Mumbai and Navi Mumbai, it was to make the scheme financially viable for the commercial private sector. As slum redevelopment also comprises high-rise housing development, some professionals view the lowering of standards as discrimination against the lower-income groups.

Source: Adusumilli and Shekdar, 2004 (see CD-Rom)

Several areas requiring changes were identified, but it took 25 years for this advice to be heeded by the authorities concerned and for significant changes to be made (Payne, 2001, p11).

Box 2.7 Million Houses Programme in Colombo, Sri Lanka

The programme piloted a number of upgrading projects in Colombo from 1978 to 1984. During that period, several innovative approaches were developed to improve the living environments of the urban poor in Colombo. These included the following:

- The development of procedures for the declaration of all settlements identified for upgrading and relocation as special projects under Urban Development Authority (UDA) legislation.
- Normal building regulations (Rules of the Housing and Town Improvement Ordinance of 1915 and UDA Regulations) were relaxed in the declared special project areas in order to make the housing affordable for the poor, and to allow low-income households to stay in the same locations and continue their livelihoods.
- Innovative participatory methods were introduced in land regulation, the provision of infrastructure, house building and other social development programmes.

Source: SEVANATHA, 2001 (see CD-Rom)

Box 2.8 Unauthorized settlements in Tanzania

Official statements point out that 70 per cent of Dar es Salaam's residents live in informal settlements. This is possibly an understatement. This percentage was determined in the late 1970s as part of the data collected for the preparation of the Dar es Salaam Master Plan of 1979. Since then, informal settlements have grown extensively, taking in even high-income households, while the planned sector has hardly grown. Data collected for property tax purposes indicate that there are 350,000 properties in Dar es Salaam. An estimated 60,000 of these (based on the number of surveyed plots since the colonial era) are on planned land. This suggests that some 83 per cent of all properties in the city are in informal settlements.

Source: Kironde, 2004 (see CD-Rom)

WHY REGULATE? THE PROS AND CONS OF REGULATION

Regulatory frameworks are intended to ensure the systematic growth of cities and towns that meet the development needs of different parts of the economy and different sections of society. They are also intended to ensure public health and safety, and can thus be regarded as tools for the greater good of society. However, as is common with many good intentions, regulatory frameworks can have both positive and negative outcomes.

Positive aspects of regulation

Regulatory frameworks are intended to accomplish the following:

Achieve orderly land development

The large and increasing number of unauthorized urban land developments testifies to the widespread failure of existing regulatory frameworks to control the form of urban growth. The unregulated and unauthorized development of land often occurs even in middle- and high-income residential neighbourhoods, as well as in areas zoned for other purposes. However, appropriate regulatory frameworks *can* help to ensure orderly land development, which is essential for the efficient and equitable growth of urban areas.

Regulatory frameworks are intended to ensure the systematic growth of cities and towns that meet the development needs of different parts of the economy and different sections of society

Facilitate efficient land management

Urban land is a valuable and finite resource which is becoming increasingly scarce in most developing countries. Efficient land management makes for the optimum use of land and is therefore of paramount importance for a continued supply at affordable cost, in particular for the poor. Regulatory frameworks based on the knowledge, understanding and acceptance of existing practices and land delivery mechanisms can help ensure efficient land management and the environmentally sound use of land. This means that definitions of efficiency need to take into account how people actually perceive and use land, rather than just using economic considerations.

Attract and guide inward and local investment

Investors are averse to risk. They will therefore not commit themselves if they have reason to believe that their investments may be threatened. A major source of risk is uncertainty. If potential investors are not informed about the relevant regulatory requirements to which they must conform in order to obtain a reasonable return on their investment, they may not be willing to invest. At the same time, such regulatory requirements must themselves be seen as permitting a reasonable return on investment, while also protecting the public interest in terms of social welfare, public health and the environment. For housing developers, high official standards plus complex regulations and administrative procedures increase both the risks and the costs, making it increasingly difficult for the private sector to meet the housing needs of lower-income groups. When assessing the costs and risks involved in conforming to regulatory guidelines, it is important to apply market-based costs. These will be the ones that households and developers have to meet unless governments distort investment decisions by subsidizing selected costs. Such subsidies may well be necessary, but can easily be captured by higher-income groups, may not be fully quantified and are often not sustainable. Regulatory frameworks need to balance these conflicting considerations.

Maximize public revenues

If governments, at both central and local levels, are to meet the expectations of citizens and deliver on their socio-economic development mandates, they must have a sound revenue base. This is especially so in urban areas, where service provision is a primary responsibility of local authorities. Regulatory frameworks that enable governments to effectively manage urban development can facilitate the use of land-based and other forms of taxation in mobilizing financial resources for service delivery and other essential functions by local authorities.

Protect the environment and public health

Just as in rural areas, protecting the urban environment and public health is essential to the well-being of individuals, communities and society as a whole (see Box 2.9). Inadequate sanitation, for instance, frequently leads to people defecating in open spaces, which is a public health hazard. Stagnant water caused by inadequate drainage can likewise be a source of disease. And it is not just the outdoor environment that is important. Many people also get exposed to indoor air pollution caused by inefficient cooking and heating, which harms and kills many women and small children. Simple rules regarding the evacuation of smoke can greatly diminish this risk.

Mitigate the impact of disasters

Usually, it is the low-income settlements of developing country cities that are hardest hit when natural disasters – such as earthquakes, floods, storms or landslides – strike. This is partly because people are forced to build their houses on environmentally hazardous sites such as steep hillsides prone to landslides, swamps or flood-prone areas, as all safe land is either already developed or too expensive.

Help the poor access improved housing, services and credit

Regulatory frameworks can facilitate access to improved housing, services and credit for people living in poverty in existing informal settlements. They can likewise help the poor acquire affordable legal housing through new development. For example, standards stipulate the level to which officially acceptable housing and infrastructure development should conform. Making them appropriate to the needs of the poor, and also affordable, will improve access. Equally, permitting modest initial standards of development will enable the poor to enter the legal housing market and improve their housing over time. Regulatory frameworks can also prevent discrimination and barriers to accessing credit for poor women and men.

Box 2.9 Striking a balance

In many countries it is clear that where regulations are excessive (or unknown, unenforceable and inappropriate), they are usually disregarded by the bulk of the population. The research has demonstrated the need for planners to simplify the framework and make it more accessible to ordinary people. This does not, however, mean discarding all regulations, which would simply lead to anarchy and chaos. In order to strike a balance, it is important to maintain the most critical regulations that maintain health and safety and ensure a degree of access. The Lesotho team found, for example, that the following regulatory factors needed to be maintained:

- Maintenance of *access routes* to enable the provision of services either before or after settlement of the area.
- Regulation of *sanitation*, particularly pit latrine and standpipe quality.
- Reservation of *public spaces* for the future development of schools, health services, community centres, graveyards, public parks and commercial centres.
- Preservation of reasonable plot sizes *in certain parts of the peri-urban area* where multiple livelihood strategies are important.

Most important, the Lesotho case demonstrated the need for the regulatory framework to be implemented in a manner that is transparent and inclusive, where both traditional authorities, individual landowners (or users) and government experts are involved at a local level. All these stakeholders should have a say in which regulations are maintained and how they are modified over time.

Source: Hall, 2004 (see CD-Rom)

Protect occupants from unscrupulous developers

The regulatory framework can protect tenants or future owners from problems caused by careless or exploitative methods of development. Such problems may include excessive site development or inadequate daylighting, access or drainage etc.

Minimize harmful externalities

Many land uses generate externalities or spill-over effects which can affect whole neighbourhoods. Public authorities regulate to minimize such harmful effects as pollution, congestion, overcrowding, noise, smell and so forth and to prevent the growth of inappropriate urban forms.

Allow for common land uses

It is observable that where there is a lack of regulation, individual households tend to maximize private interests, ignoring land uses necessary for the community such as roads, open spaces and land for social services. Regulatory frameworks usually specify the amount of land to be set aside for such uses, and the standards that must be observed.

Negative aspects of regulation

The negative aspects of regulation are generally the inverse of the positive aspects, and include the following risks.

Over-regulating and therefore discouraging investment

Regulation that is too prescriptive or proscriptive in what is allowed or not allowed may be a deterrent to potential investors. Excessive controls may make it impossible to obtain a reasonable return on investment or use the development in ways the developer or residents would want to.

Regulation that is too prescriptive or proscriptive in what is allowed and not allowed may be a deterrent to potential investors

Imposing regulations, standards or administrative procedures that increase costs to levels which many people cannot afford

As explained earlier, existing regulatory frameworks in many developing country cities were inherited or imported from foreign nations without adaptation, or were designed for an affluent minority. The urban poor majority are thus compelled to comply with regulations, standards and administrative procedures that are not only inappropriate to their circumstances, but are also beyond their means (see Box 2.10).

Failing to reflect the cultural priorities of different groups, especially in the ways people perceive and use dwellings and open space

Official norms often prevent people from using their plots for home-based enterprises (HBEs), inhibit multi-occupancy, or insist on larger plot sizes than people can afford. Such restrictions commonly force the poor to seek shelter in informal settlements and prevent others from moving out of them.

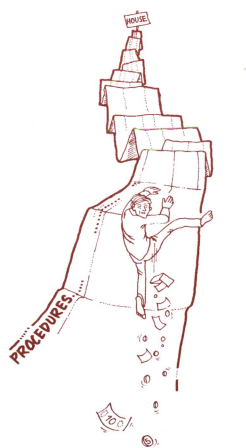

The poor are often compelled to comply with regulations, standards and administrative procedures that are not only inappropriate to their circumstances, but are also beyond their means

Box 2.10 Possible constraints represented by administrative procedures in different countries

Studies conducted in six countries under the Regulatory Guidelines for Affordable Shelter project found administrative procedures to be the greatest constraint to people trying to access new legal shelter. The reasons included the following:

India

- Administrative procedures are too varied and complicated, and few people understand what they are supposed to do due to lack of clarity and information.
- There are severe delays in the processing of applications.
- Bribes and informal charges are levied during the procedures amounting to 15 per cent or more of total project costs and, if not paid, lead to consequent delays and escalation in costs.
- Formal costs, such as the costs of obtaining legal development permission and utility connections, are too high.
- Costs per unit area of land are higher for smaller plots, as many of the services bear a minimum charge irrespective of the plot size. The poor thus bear the heaviest cost burdens.
- Obtaining development permission takes anything up to four years for an individual household.
- In Navi Mumbai, even once building plans have been approved, a revalidation of the plans is required every year until completion. This involves more visits to the public office and more payments of nominal fees. Therefore, even if they begin the process legally, many people end up making additions and alterations to their properties illegally.

Lesotho

- Administrative procedures are largely unknown and not followed by the majority of the population.
- The majority of the population live in peri-urban areas where the formal system barely functions. Here they are able to access land efficiently under the customary system, which is quicker and well established, although it is not technically part of the modern regulatory framework.
- The procedures are over-centralized, especially the requirement of ministerial approval for leases, which results in endless delays. This is the major constraint to accessing legal housing.

Note: For all reports on case study countries, see CD-Rom

Tanzania

- Many of the provisions of the regulatory framework are old and are inappropriate to the context.
- Standards, regulations and procedures are not well known to the public, or even to officials themselves. Information cannot be accessed easily as documentation is often out of print, hard to find and/or is in English.
- The authorities in charge of implementing the regulatory framework are too centralized, leading to delays and high direct and indirect costs.
- Inappropriate procedures mean that eight years can elapse before land earmarked for development can be translated into land plots for allocation. Equally, to get a right of occupancy takes so long that the majority of landowners have no title several years after the allocation of land.

Institutionalizing corruption through 'fees' for non-enforcement

The high costs involved in complying with regulatory requirements make many of those required to do so turn to illegal means to get those responsible for enforcement to turn a blind eye. Illegal payments to officials are difficult to stop once established and inhibit attempts to improve urban governance.

Creating overlapping or contradictory conditions which expose developers or individuals to the risk of conforming to one regulation or standard and therefore contravening another

Changes to regulatory frameworks commonly involve the addition of new standards, regulations or procedures to existing regulatory obligations without any revisions to those already in force. Overlaps and contradictions are thus not unusual, with the result that complying to a newer regulation may mean contravening an older one. This can easily render residents and developers vulnerable to demands for bribes from officials.

The importance of regulation in improving and preventing substandard urban settlements

Regulatory frameworks are important in improving existing substandard urban settlements and preventing the development of new ones in the future for two reasons:

1 First, they are a key factor in the ability (or inability) of poor people to conform to official requirements of legality and therefore full citizenship.

2 Second, they are within the remit of governments to formulate and revise. At a time when the influence of globalization and the private sector in most facets of economic life is greater than ever, the importance of regulatory frameworks is comparatively greater. It is therefore vital that they are relevant to the social, cultural, economic and environmental conditions of a particular place at a particular time.

WHO MAKES THE RULES?

The responsibility for formulating, enforcing and monitoring regulatory frameworks differs from country to country. Standards, regulations and administrative procedures are created by different regulatory bodies (eg parliamentary bodies, government departments or statutory boards), or other bodies or persons with delegated authority, such as an administrative agency or an office holder. They are commonly enabled by a specific statute.

Many of the regulatory requirements in force in cities and towns are made by central governments and enforced by local authorities, governmental boards or local committees etc. The responsibility for formulating, enforcing and monitoring planning regulations and standards may also vary considerably between and within different levels of government (see Box 2.11). While national governments are responsible for establishing the legal framework for regulatory

Box 2.11 Multi-level regulations and change

In India, regulatory frameworks are local (municipal) concerns, whereas in most other countries they are more a national-level responsibility. For example, in Navi Mumbai, the Development Authority for Navi Mumbai (CIDCO) and the Navi Mumbai Municipal Corporation – the two local development bodies – are responsible for granting development permissions and allotting plots, while the regulatory mechanism originates at the state government level with the Town Planning Act provisions. There are also over-riding state and national regulations, such as those imposed from an environmental point of view. Such intricate overlaps and over-rides should be taken into consideration when carrying out a regulatory audit or reviewing regulatory frameworks.

Source: Adusumilli and Shekdar, 2004 (see CD-Rom)

guidelines, provincial and municipal governments invariably possess delegated or discretionary powers in order to ensure that such guidelines are relevant to local conditions, needs and resources. This makes it difficult to enforce or change regulatory guidelines, since there will be more groups to consult and persuade. This can also create inertia within the civil service and provide those groups benefiting from the status quo with an excuse not to change. In cases where standards, regulations or administrative procedures are established by central government, the scope for local authorities to change them may also be severely restricted.

Although governments are ultimately responsible for establishing and revising regulatory frameworks, many other stakeholders have an interest in ensuring that they are relevant to the needs of all sections of the urban population, especially the poor. These include NGOs, CBOs, professional groups and other civil society associations which represent the needs of the poor. Their ability to mobilize people can help generate momentum for change which would otherwise be slower and less effective. The relevant responsibilities applicable in different contexts can be assessed by completing a table on institutional responsibilities or undertaking a stakeholder analysis (available on the CD-Rom).

WHOSE INTERESTS IS THE REGULATORY FRAMEWORK DESIGNED TO SERVE?

Regulatory frameworks, as stated earlier, are intended to serve the interests of society at large by ensuring orderly development along with public health and safety. However, many of the legal and regulatory frameworks controlling development in developing country urban areas are of little practical relevance to the prevailing socio-economic situation. The planning regulations and building standards in force will, in many cases, have been derived from contexts that bear little relationship to the realities faced by poor households. They will also have been designed mainly for, and by, an affluent minority that has little in common with the urban poor majority.

Those who originally formulated the regulatory frameworks rarely anticipated what can now be found in nearly all cases: a dual economy comprised of formal and informal sectors. Most of the urban poor earn their livelihoods through informal sector income-generating activities that are predominantly located in the informal settlements in which the majority of them live. Regulatory requirements that adversely affect their shelter needs therefore also impact negatively on their economic circumstances, making it more difficult for governments to achieve poverty-reduction goals. Regulatory obligations set down by central and local governments are seen by most as irrelevant, and are thus simply ignored. The costs they represent are also unaffordable in terms of money and time. Moreover, the poor do not have the other resources needed to fulfil them, such as information and contacts.

The political aspect of regulatory frameworks is rarely given the attention it deserves. Planning regulations and standards are almost always formulated by professionals and therefore tend to reflect the perceptions, and protect the interests of, the affluent minority. To some extent, they seek to impose standards and regulations which require anyone seeking permission to develop land to meet the norms they regard as reflecting their own definition of acceptability. If some social groups cannot afford to conform to these, then, by implication, they have no right to be in the city at all. Such socially divisive features are not, of course, expressed openly, but are an integral factor in many regulatory regimes. Administrative procedures are similarly not bureaucratically neutral, but designed to ensure that all those who fail to conform are subject to the full weight of the law. They also expose non-conforming developers, both formal and informal, to exploitation by local officials who are able to extract money in return for turning a blind eye. The key issue is, therefore, whose interests is the regulatory framework designed to serve?

If it is to meet basic development objectives, a regulatory framework should enable access to appropriate, affordable services by all urban dwellers, including the poorest, through trade-offs or subsidies if necessary. One way of achieving this is to require developers to reallocate a proportion of their profits from high-income housing, commercial and industrial development towards part of the costs of housing or services for the urban poor, providing that the proportion reallocated does not prevent developers from obtaining a reasonable return on their investment. Regulatory frameworks which permit modest standards and simple procedures are likely to facilitate such approaches.

KEY QUESTIONS

- How are planning regulations, planning standards and administrative procedures defined in your country/city?

- Are planning regulations, planning standards and administrative procedures in your city the same for upgrading existing settlements and new development?

- Are regulatory guidelines readily available and easily understood by officials and the general public, especially the poor? In what ways are they disseminated?

- Are the standards of development applicable in formal and unauthorized urban settlements very different? If so, in what ways?

- Are planning regulations, planning standards and administrative procedures in your city based on inherited or imported norms and needs?

- Do planning regulations, standards and administrative procedures in your country apply nationally or are there regional variations?

- Are there dual legal systems (traditional and modern) involved in the regulation?

- Who has regulatory responsibilities in your country/city and what are they responsible for?

- Are there any regulations which contradict each other?

- What proportion of households in your city/country comply with all planning regulations, standards and administrative procedures? Of households which do not comply, which standards, regulations or procedures are most commonly ignored?

- How long does it normally take and how many stages need to be negotiated to register a plot of land and obtain permission to build on it?

- What proportion of low-income households are able to obtain formal credit in your city?

- What subsidies are available to low-income households and how many households receive these annually?

- Who *initiates*, who *formulates* and who *implements* regulatory frameworks in your country/city?

3 HOW DO REGULATORY FRAMEWORKS AFFECT THE URBAN POOR?

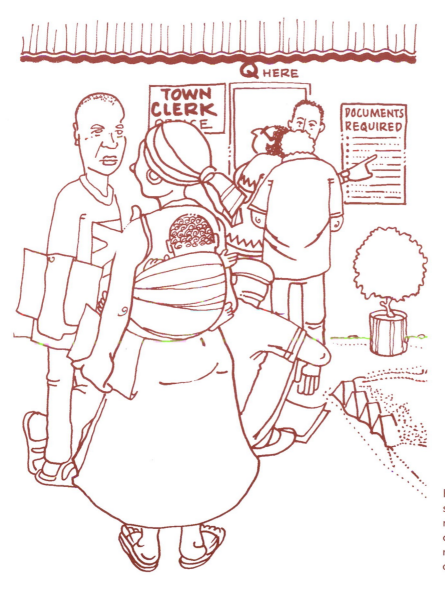

Following planning standards and regulations will often consume the scarce resources at the disposal of the poor

The present impact of regulatory frameworks on poor people in urban settlements is generally negative and adversely affects their livelihoods for the following reasons:

- Regulations generally prevent developments that meet the needs and budgets of the urban poor, such as incremental development.
- Regulations may prevent the poor from generating incomes in residential areas.
- Standards are rarely related to costs and are often unaffordable to the poor.
- Procedures can be time-consuming and costly.
- Costly bribes are often the only way to obtain required documentation.
- Information is often difficult to access. Even when available, information is often unintelligible to the non-professional.
- Enforcement of the regulations may expose residents to exploitation by gangs or unscrupulous officials.

There are significant costs, both monetary and non-monetary, attached to complying with regulatory frameworks. In addition, uniform regulatory levies create an inordinate burden on the poor, resulting in more resistance than compliance to regulations. Regulatory frameworks impact differently on different groups. For example, their impact on women living in poverty in informal settlements is different to that on men in the same circumstances (see Box 3.1).

The poor have, however, not remained passive victims of unfavourable planning regulations, standards and administrative procedures. Instead, they have taken action to establish alternative regulatory regimes related to their own economic, social, cultural and environmental needs and priorities. Informal developers, sometimes working in conjunction with customary authorities, have been quick to capitalize on these to develop settlements which now represent the majority of all new land development in many cities and towns. However, as competition for land increases with urban growth, prices have risen to the level at which even middle-income households are finding it increasingly difficult to conform to official requirements. While this has reduced the social stigma suffered by the poor majority, it has not helped in changing inappropriate regulatory frameworks.

Box 3.1 Gender: a cross-cutting issue

Gender is a cross-cutting issue which impacts on all matters related to housing. Even in the same household, men and women have very different relationships to land, property and housing. Men and women, because of their different roles in everyday life, experience human settlements and urban poverty in different ways, have different needs and priorities, and are faced with different opportunities and constraints in building their livelihoods. In order for urban development policies to be appropriate and successful, it is therefore essential that the differences in men's and women's experiences, needs and priorities be fully recognized.

Women around the world are frequently discriminated against in statutory, customary and even informal tenure systems and therefore find it difficult to access land, property and housing rights (Benschop, 2002; FAO, 2002). Women, and women-headed households in particular, are also over-represented among the poor and vulnerable sectors of society. Inappropriate regulatory frameworks that increase the costs of legal housing options may therefore have a disproportionate impact on women who are then forced to rely on informal markets for housing (Beall and Kanji, 1998).

Women may also face greater obstacles to meeting and complying with inappropriate standards, regulations and administrative procedures due to their socially prescribed roles. For instance, in contexts where women's interactions are restricted beyond the household and with non-relatives they will face greater difficulties following complex, multi-staged administrative procedures.

Inappropriate regulatory frameworks may also constrain the options open to women to build a livelihood. For instance, home-based enterprises are often more important for women as income sources due to the need to balance domestic chores with employment, or due to their restricted movements beyond the home. Equally, in settlements where there is inadequate access to infrastructure, such as running water and sewerage systems, extra burdens are likely to be imposed on women's already limited time, energy and resources in their responsibility for domestic chores (Beall, 2000; Moser, 1987a; Moser, 1987b).

However, well-designed and gender-aware regulatory frameworks can increase the options of both women and men for building their livelihoods; increase access to income and other resources; and can help empower women, allowing them to increase their standing and powers of decision-making within and beyond the home. In fact, many countries have recently begun to enshrine equal rights to land, housing and property for men and women in their statutory legislation, but cultural practices are taking longer to catch up.

Note: For a checklist of things to keep in mind for gender-aware research, see CD-Rom.
Source: Evelyn Tehrani

Regulatory guidelines for different aspects of housing and urban development affect the poor in different ways. Thus, the ability to access land, services, housing and credit will be directly and indirectly influenced by regulatory and procedural requirements. Where these raise costs, increase risk, delay returns on investment or impose terms and conditions which the poor are unable to satisfy, they will be forced into various forms of unauthorized development. Blaming them for non-conformity is therefore tantamount to blaming the victim for the crime. Some of the ways in which regulatory regimes for these components affect access and livelihoods for the poor are summarized below.

LAND

Lack of access to land is a major impediment to the meaningful participation of poor women and men in the urban economy, and the achievement of poverty reduction objectives. Access to land is also required for the development of new housing in urban areas.

The high price of urban land and the low incomes of many households makes land the largest cost component of legal housing in most cities.[1] In addition, urban land markets in developing

Box 3.2 Inappropriate standards in Tanzania

The report on Tanzania highlighted that the planning standards adopted for planning schemes demarcate plots of land which are too large, and allocate more land to roads than is necessary. These factors in this context mean that:

- density is too low on prime urban land;
- the supply of planned land in the few planning schemes that exist is restricted;
- higher-income groups are likely to poach these areas from low-income households; and
- a lot of land is left unnecessarily undeveloped or underdeveloped.

In the Kinyerezi planning scheme in Dar es Salaam implemented in the 1990s, a total of 3600 plots were planned and surveyed. If a minimum plot size of 288m^2 had been adopted throughout (and this is considered generous in many countries), and if the land set aside for roads had been reduced by 50 per cent, the total number of plots that could have been realized from the same area would have been 15,000. These plots could have been afforded by a wider spectrum of households, and the large numbers would have meant that there was more supply for everybody.

Source: Kironde, 2004 (see CD-Rom)

countries are often dominated by a rich and powerful minority who manipulate prices and further constrain access to land for the urban poor majority. The fact that over 60 per cent of the population of Nairobi live in informal settlements occupying less than 5 per cent of the total residential land (ITDG–EA, 2001), and more than 50 per cent of the population of Mumbai are slum dwellers living on only 8 per cent of the land (Lall, 2001), clearly illustrates the difficulty poor households have in gaining access to land in the two cities. It is also indicative of distorted and dysfunctional land markets as well as inappropriate regulatory frameworks.

Spatial requirements in urban planning regulations commonly make legal land development impossible for the poor. In most cases they cannot afford the stipulated minimum plot sizes. Excessively large plot sizes, wide roads and areas for public open space also raise the unit costs of land, reduce densities and impose higher maintenance and transport costs, forcing the urban poor into informal settlements, many of which use land more efficiently and creatively (see Box 3.2). High standards also increase the costs of upgrading projects and may require more households to be displaced. Greater consideration needs to be given to the

The relationships between the formal and the informal sectors are complex and symbiotic: most people function in both. Removing 'illegal' development is a simplistic response that may adversely affect the formal economy

relationship between standards, regulations, costs, needs and resources (both public and private) if these issues are to be resolved.

SECURITY OF TENURE

Urban land tenure issues are highly complex, and cannot be defined simply in terms of legal or illegal, formal or informal. There may be several forms of legal land tenure and property rights in many urban areas (eg statutory, customary and religious), together with a range of extra-legal categories (eg squatting, unauthorized land subdivisions, houses constructed or expanded in contravention of official norms, or without official permits etc). Most people therefore live within a continuum in which some aspects of their housing are legal and others are not. It is essential to identify the range of statutory, customary and informal tenure categories in a town or city so that the consequences of urban policy on different tenure sub-markets can be anticipated (Payne, 2001).

The high cost of land resulting from market forces and restrictive regulatory frameworks tends to exclude large numbers of people, especially the poor, from obtaining legal access to land and shelter. This is often reinforced by rigid tenure policies which seek to remove unauthorized settlements rather than address the constraints on obtaining legal shelter.

The scale of non-formal tenure developments can be considered largely as a reflection of the extent to which tenure policies and regulatory frameworks have failed to reflect the needs and resources of the urban population within the broader economic environment. Inappropriate policies therefore force households into the very unauthorized settlements that governments seek to prevent. This issue can only be addressed by central governments as they create the legal, financial, institutional and political framework within which urban development takes place.

Secure tenure is a necessary, but not sufficient, condition for creating sustainable urban livelihoods. Given the complex nature of

tenure categories in most cities, giving some households full individual titles is more likely to increase existing distortions in urban land markets and encourage further informal development. Moreover, experience has shown, time and again, that the urban poor either willingly sell or otherwise lose their land when given individual title. The most effective approach is therefore to widen the range of legal options and increase the short-term security for residents in customary or unauthorized settlements until such time as more formal options can be extended to all categories. This can be achieved by implementing an incremental approach in which all unauthorized settlements are provided with protection from forced eviction for a minimum period of, say, 6 to 12 months, following which communal land rights and eventually some form of statutory tenure can be provided.[2]

Secure and affordable housing is a pre-condition for creating sustainable urban livelihoods. The most effective approach is to widen the range of intermediate options until formal tenure can be introduced

INFRASTRUCTURE

Urban infrastructure is essential to economic and social development in developing as well as developed countries. If it is inadequate, deteriorated or obsolete it will constrain the development of the locality, municipality or city, or even the nation. The provision of infrastructure to informal settlements in which the urban poor majority in developing countries live and work is perhaps the most basic of needs, in that a supply of clean water is absolutely necessary for life and well-being, while the lack of sanitation is a major public health hazard that causes disease, sickness and death. The lack of clean water or effective sanitation can thus discourage inward investment in urban areas (Payne, 2001, p7). Yet only 40 per cent of households in informal settlements in developing countries have access to clean water (UN-Habitat, 2003a, p11), and city-level data from 43 African cities indicate that 83 per cent of the population lack toilets that are connected to sewers; for the large cities of Asia this statistic is 55 per cent (UN-Habitat, nd).[3]

City and municipal governments are responsible for providing infrastructure to their citizens. There is, however, great variation in the extent to which they have sole responsibility for provision, shared responsibility with higher levels of government, or a supervisory and regulatory role for other service providers (including the private sector, both formal and informal, and NGO providers).[4] In most cases they are not required to provide services to informal settlements which have developed without regulatory approval. With no access to municipal services, the urban poor are compelled to pay private vendors much more for their water, compared with their affluent neighbours who are connected to municipal supplies. They also often have to pay to use latrines (see Box 3.3). What is more, they also pay for inadequate sanitation with the loss of productivity and dignity (UN-Habitat, 2003b, p6).

HOUSING

The right to adequate housing is recognized as an important component of the right to an adequate standard of living in the Universal Declaration on Human Rights of 1948.[5] However, as explained in Section 1, 'The Urbanization of Poverty', p9, the vast majority of poor urban dwellers have been unable to gain access to adequate housing largely owing to the regulatory frameworks operating in the cities and towns in which they live. This has not only denied them the environmental, health, safety and social welfare benefits of adequate legal housing, but also the chance to earn livelihoods through home-based entrepreneurial activities.

Most housing regulations and standards have been conceived with new housing development in mind, often of the type of a single

Box 3.3 Access to infrastructure by the urban poor in informal settlements

A major constraint that poor urban dwellers face in seeking to improve their livelihoods and access to legal housing is their limited access to infrastructure and services, including water supply, sanitation, drainage, garbage collection, access roads and pathways, street lighting, flood protection and public transport. They face even more problems because design and service standards are, in most cases, unaffordable and not planned for incremental upgrading. Moreover, existing procedures, rules and forms of contracting rule out the involvement of poor communities in the implementation and management of their local infrastructure. The vast majority of urban poor people living and working in informal settlements are [thus] forced to rely on small-scale private-sector and community-based service providers ... for basic urban services. But infrastructure standards and regulations typically exclude small community-based entrepreneurs who lack the capital or technology required. Yet it is precisely these enterprises that are likely to offer lower-cost services affordable by the urban poor.

Source: Majale, 2002a; Majale, 2002b (see CD-Rom)

house on its own plot. This, in itself, is unaffordable to many urban households. But increasingly, we also have to deal with rental housing that is often no more than a single room per household, or with the upgrading of existing housing that has been built outside the rules. And we often find the existing rules inadequate to deal with such cases. The big question is whether one ought to develop different standards for all these cases, or perhaps go for an absolute minimum level – for example, to guarantee public health – but allow flexibility beyond that. The starter standards developed in Jamaica, or the standards for traditional housing areas in Malawi, are moves in that direction. Other countries have opted for several levels. Kenya, for example, has Grade 1 and Grade 2 building bylaws, and Sri Lanka allows municipalities to declare certain settlements 'special project areas', where lower standards are allowed.

Previous research into housing standards (eg Yahya et al, 2001) has brought up a number of issues that ought to be considered in their revision. These are summarized below, and explained in greater length on the CD-Rom:

* Allowing incremental development both in terms of quality and of space; in the latter case, growth could be horizontal or vertical.
* Involving communities in setting housing standards and regulations.

The diversity in housing needs makes it difficult to anticipate every aspect. The key issue is how to define and protect the public interest and public health while permitting local control and variety

- Redefining the concept of a dwelling, the amount of floor space required and the permissible plot coverage.
- Paying more attention to the indoor environment, and particularly to smoke removal.
- Adopting performance standards for construction, to allow for a greater range of materials and components.
- Facilitating the adoption of innovative technologies in regulation.
- Mitigating the risk of disasters in affordable ways.

HOME-BASED ENTERPRISE

Home-based enterprises (HBEs) comprise entrepreneurial activities that take place in the home, whatever their scale. Most involve members of the household in activities which range from small-scale, part-time tasks with minimal spatial demands, to manufacturing activities that may dominate the dwelling environment. The use of residential space for HBEs is extremely widespread. HBEs can be found in between 20 and 40 per cent of properties in low-income neighbourhoods in many cities in developing countries, even though they are almost always unapproved by planning authorities. They generally take up very little space in the dwellings but, where there is little domestic space, even this can cause problems of crowding.

HBEs are expected to fulfil regulations pertaining to employment as well as housing, so they are doubly liable to official interventions. Employment regulations relate to occupational health and safety in the workplace, working conditions, work breaks, allowances, unionization, etc (Kellett and Tipple, 2000; Tipple et al, 2002).

As regulatory frameworks result in the illegality of HBEs, they tend to perpetuate the informality of employment opportunities open to the urban poor, increase the vulnerability of workers, discourage asset accumulation and constrain access to credit. Policy-makers and regulators have been highly critical of HBEs for many reasons, including the exploitation of homeworkers by middle-men and factories. It is, however, the failure to comply with regulations that gives many HBEs a competitive edge over formal sector enterprises which have to bear heavy overhead costs as a result of regulatory compliance (Singh and Kowale, 2000; Kellett and Tipple, 2000; Tipple et al, 2002). This ability to minimize overhead costs has enabled HBEs to be founded and to expand so that, in some cities, they provide an indispensable contribution to the success of formal industries (Benjamin, 1990).

Regulatory frameworks rarely take into account the fact that HBEs are very important for income and employment among low-income households. They tend to assume that people live in residential areas and work in industrial or commercial areas. The reality is not so clear-cut, and some accommodation of the need for low-cost employment and entrepreneurship is needed.

CREDIT AND FINANCE

Getting access to credit in the formal financial sector is one of the biggest problems facing the urban poor in developing countries, largely owing to prevailing fiscal and regulatory frameworks. In developed countries, financial institutions mostly base their loan decisions on individual guarantees and readily available information on borrowers' credit risks. But poor households in developing countries typically do not have acceptable collateral and guarantee mechanisms. This situation, coupled with the overall lack of information about their credit-worthiness, contributes to their virtual exclusion from formal credit markets. The situation is exacerbated by regulatory frameworks that constrain formal lending institutions from lending to the poor.

As they are not eligible for credit and finance in the formal sector, many urban poor households are forced to seek loans from informal money lenders who charge even higher interest rates than banks or other formal lending agencies, and who are ruthless in exacting repayments. Micro-finance agencies have provided loans without the requirement for collateral, but borrowing is usually restricted to short-term loans largely targeted at income-generating activities. Micro-finance institutions tend to charge high rates of interest because little, if any, collateral is available, and this makes long-term lending, even if it were available, unaffordable. However, there are also examples of innovative credit and loan systems, such as the range of urban poor funds that have been established within the Slum/Shack Dwellers International (SDI) Network, which have been designed to support community-led initiatives in housing and infrastructure provision. Funds of this kind now exist in Cambodia, India, South Africa, Zimbabwe, Namibia, the Philippines, Thailand and a number of other countries.

One of the most challenging areas with respect to finance is accessing the capital needed to fund large-scale, community-led urban upgrading initiatives. Formal banks have proved reluctant to lend to such schemes as they are often unclear as to how to analyse the risks involved, and rarely have the systems in place to manage such loans. The banks' risk-aversion is often reflected in their demands that planning and building regulations be met in full even where it is generally acknowledged that other developments, including many initiated and managed by government agencies, are using more flexible standards. In 2003, a new facility – the Community-Led Infrastructure Finance Facility (CLIFF) – was established by Cities Alliance to help bridge the gap that has existed in such financing. CLIFF provides venture capital to organizations of the urban poor which are taking the lead in developing upgrading schemes. CLIFF is being piloted in India and will shortly be established in Kenya as well (ACHR, 2002; Boonyabancha, 2003; McLeod, 2001a; McLeod, 2001b; McLeod, 2001c; McLeod, 2001d; McLeod, 2002; McLeod, 2003).

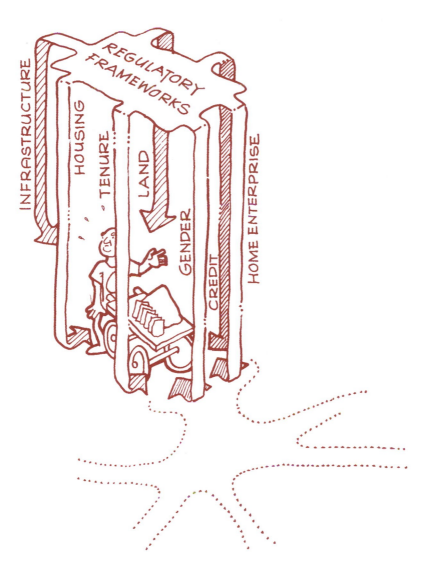

In formulating regulatory frameworks, professionals seek to create efficient, planned environments based on their own perceptions. In reality, such rules and regulations can act as barriers that restrict options for the poor and their ability to conform

WHY HAVE REGULATIONS THAT ADVERSELY AFFECT THE POOR NOT BEEN CHANGED?

Regulatory frameworks exert a significant influence over the costs and benefits of urban development. Where a regulatory framework was established to protect the interests of a political, economic, social or other elite, it can be expected that the elite will seek to maintain the status quo and protect their advantages. Groups resisting change may include politicians, government officials, professionals and NGOs (see Box 3.4). Each may have benign motives, including the desire to provide a higher standard of living

> ## Box 3.4 Institutional culture in the public sector as a constraint on change
>
> A national training needs assessment for the shelter sector in India during the late 1980s found that the institutional culture among public sector professionals was extremely conservative and resistant to change. This was partly due to a bureaucratic environment which discouraged initiative or risk-taking and reinforced the view that 'the professionals know best'. Furthermore, the poor pay and career structure of the civil service meant that the brightest students preferred to work in the private sector, leaving less ambitious or imaginative colleagues to apply for posts in urban planning and management agencies. Although the notion of public service attracted many capable staff, their lack of exposure to the rigours of the market and the need for resources to be used efficiently meant that they were not well placed to initiate change.
>
> For those further down the professional ladder who had more direct contact with the communities they were responsible for, vested interests often took a more personal form. The more rigorous the planning standards, regulations and administrative procedures they were required to enforce, the greater the opportunities they had for extorting 'considerations' from those who breached them.

Source: Payne, 2001 (see CD-Rom)

for the population, or at least those whose interests they represent. They may see themselves as upholding standards of decency or law and order. They may also wish to protect the poor from the rigours of market forces, which often drive standards down.

On the other hand, change-resistant groups may be seeking personal advantages from bribes, commissions or other benefits. They may also see unregulated development and informal settlements as a challenge to their professional authority. Both the benign and ulterior motives act as constraints on change. Finally, inertia may explain why all or some of these groups resist change. For example, politicians may not consider that there are any political advantages (eg votes) to be gained from pursuing change, especially if it involves reducing standards which were once imposed by foreigners (see Box 3.5).

Regulatory frameworks that inhibit settlement upgrading may be based on a concern that it would encourage further urban population growth and more informal settlements, or that it is simply too complicated. Such fears may be justified if the standards adopted for upgrading are high and large subsidies are provided to meet them. The effect of such dramatic changes raises property

Box 3.5 Constraints on implementing change in case study countries

India

- Frequent changes in bureaucratic and managerial personnel in planning agencies.
- Governmental lethargy and apathy.
- Lack of interest in promoting housing for the poor rather than profit-making proposals among existing associations of developers and housing professionals – architects, planners and engineers.
- Reluctance among authorities to accept changes that will result in reduced revenues or involve extra administrative procedures or responsibilities.
- The time required to follow up and effect recommendations involving statutory changes that need approval from higher levels of government.

Tanzania

- Bureaucratic inertia concerning change.
- A failure to recognize the true costs imposed by the current regulatory framework.
- Inability to build an adequate constituency of support for proposed changes.
- Regulatory reforms are not considered a high priority in a context where many other reforms are underway.

Lesotho

- A general sense of bureaucratic inertia in government, resulting in *any reforms in any sector* taking years to implement.
- A fear of 'rocking the boat', implying that people who took the initiative to bring about changes risked creating resentment from those opposed to change, and in doing so put their own jobs in jeopardy.
- A feeling that taking the initiative was risky, as any 'mistakes' might bear a political cost, particularly in terms of one's position and future in the civil service.
- Other priorities result in less immediate concerns – such as the reform of administrative procedures – being indefinitely shelved.

Note: For all reports on case study countries, see CD-Rom

values, which in turn encourages many people to sell their properties and maybe repeat the process in the hope of a further windfall. By upgrading to a modest initial level and working with local communities on meeting their own priorities, such risks can be minimized.

Box 3.6 Landowners' suspicions of proposals to regulate their land in Dar es Salaam

One of the objectives of the regulatory framework project was to identify an area in order to implement recommendations from the research in a pilot scheme. In Dar es Salaam, the identified area was adjacent to the planned area in which the research for the regulatory framework project was carried out. The area is known as Zimbili, in the Kinyerezi ward in the municipality of Ilala.

Several public meetings were held between the landowners in the area and the regulatory framework project team. The latter also included officials from Ilala Municipal Council. Contrary to expectations, no amount of arguments could convince the landowners to allow the pilot project to be implemented in their area. The pilot project aimed at planning the area with the landowners, making the necessary adjustments to the land parcels to provide for regularity, and roads and other public uses. At the various meetings, the landowners said or seemed to believe that:

- the proposed project had a hidden agenda to deprive them of their land;
- the project had funds (possibly from some donor agency) which the project protagonists intended to pocket rather than spend for the benefit of the landowners; and
- there had been several past unfulfilled promises or actions, emanating from the government, that had had adverse consequences for the landowners, and the pilot scheme was likely to be one of those.

The landowners insisted on one of two approaches: the payment of compensation to any landowner who suffered loss of property as a result of the project; or that there should be no intervention whatsoever.

For the regulatory framework project, this was very disappointing, and points to at least three areas of consideration:

1 The need to involve the grass-roots population on board in any land-use schemes.
2 The need to convince landowners that the benefits of being within the legal framework outweigh continuing with the present legally uncertain situation.
3 How to undo the damage done in the past by the government to the landowners and the general public.

It may have been advantageous, as well, to have had an enforceable bylaw in place before attempting to convince the landowners.

Source: Kironde, 2004 (see CD-Rom)

Concerns are often voiced that to provide affordable new housing for the poor will only encourage urban growth. However, international experience shows that people move to urban areas for primarily economic or security reasons rather than for housing. It is the increasing gap between land and housing prices and household incomes which forces many people into unauthorized settlements. Reducing the cost of entry to the legal land and housing market can reduce the need for future slums and help in efforts to reduce poverty. Ensuring that the regulatory framework assists this process can make a major contribution to meeting these objectives.

The particular combinations of groups resisting changes to regulatory frameworks will vary from time to time and place to place (see Boxes 3.6 and 3.7). Similarly, their reasons for opposing change will vary with the circumstances. Such reasons might include bureaucratic inertia, a lack of political will, lobbying by powerful vested-interest groups, a lack of local champions for change, or a lack of realistic alternatives. Over time, other groups may find ways of benefiting directly or indirectly from the status quo, creating a coalition of interest groups resistant to change. Identifying the specific combination applicable at any time and to any place is a pre-condition for achieving change.

The next section of this manual deals with ways of addressing the regulatory constraints on upgrading existing settlements and improving access to new legal shelter.

Box 3.7 Why change was difficult to achieve in Mavoko

- Community members were largely unaware of the specific legislation that needed to be changed, but they were very clear about what effects they wanted to have changed.
- Community members pointed out that making a case for change was difficult as they could not state exactly which regulation, standard or administrative procedure they wanted changed. They also blamed a lack of unity at the grass-roots level for their inability to influence change.
- Professionals felt constrained by the fact that most of the changes they felt were necessary would have to undergo a revision of some statute or act, a process which requires consensus-building and takes a lot of time.
- Municipal officers were conscious of the effort required to effect any changes to regulatory frameworks, especially with the deficiency in the capacity to enforce such changes.

Source: ITDG–EA, 2003 (see CD-Rom)

KEY QUESTIONS

- Are the regulatory guidelines for your country relevant to the needs and resources of the poor?

- How do the poor in your country/city view the regulations: as relevant/irrelevant, protective/obstructive, etc?

- In what ways do the guidelines prevent the poor from generating incomes or accessing land?

- What sort of actions have the poor taken to establish alternative regulatory regimes?

- What lessons might be drawn from these alternatives when considering regulatory reform?

- How do spatial urban planning requirements make legal land development difficult for the poor?

- How do land tenure policies constrain access to legal shelter?

- What are the gender implications of the existing regulatory regime?

- Which groups in your country/city are opposing changes to regulatory frameworks?

- What are the reasons for their opposition?

- What percentage of households in your country/city can afford to construct housing that meets the existing regulatory requirements?

- What kind of pressure groups exist in your country/city seeking changes in regulations?

- What is the political/bureaucratic attitude towards changes in regulations?

- What forms of resident organizations are there, particularly among the low-income groups, such as political organizations, lobby organizations, advocacy organizations, etc?

4 REVIEWING REGULATORY FRAMEWORKS

The street is better for our trade than the shopping mall ... we have higher passing trade and lower overheads

As urban areas grow and change, so regulatory frameworks will need to be reviewed to ensure they meet changing needs and resources. A sure sign that a review is needed is when the proportion of unauthorized housing and urban development becomes significant. Where that proportion is also increasing relative to officially planned urban developments, the need for a review becomes urgent.

Of course, there may be many reasons for the growth of unauthorized settlements. One problem may be that the range of affordable and appropriate options is too limited. Such a restricted or 'closed' supply system reduces the possibilities of households with different needs being able to find the form of housing they need at a price they can afford. For example, as in Figure 4.1, a household may be faced with a limited range of options for obtaining land, services, finance, materials and labour within the formal supply system. Under such conditions members of the household are forced to look outside the formal housing market. At the same time, the groups who control the restricted range of options have no incentive to adapt what they provide since they enjoy an effective monopoly. This applies irrespective of whether the supply system is dominated by the public or private sector. In this way, a restricted supply system is unlikely to meet the needs of an existing population *or* adapt to meet future needs. Conversely, an open system, as shown in Figure 4.2, in which there is a range of suppliers all competing to meet needs will enable existing households to find what they need and adapt to changing needs.

Moving from a closed to an open supply system raises the need to determine priorities. For example, if a review of the supply system indicated that the major constraint to accessing legal shelter is a

FIGURE 4.1
Closed or restricted housing supply system

Source: Based on Turner, 1990

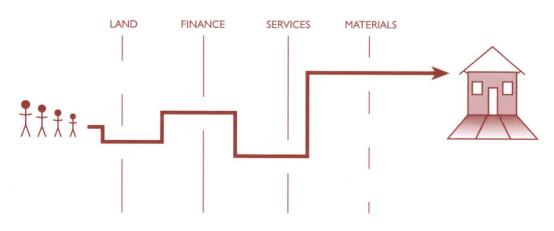

LAND   FINANCE   SERVICES   MATERIALS

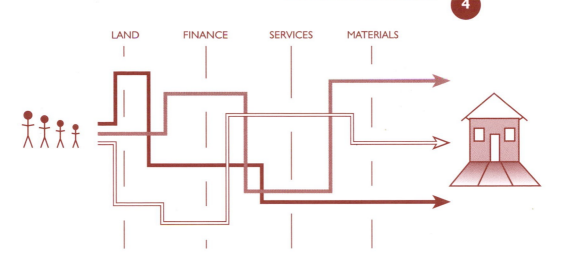

LAND   FINANCE   SERVICES   MATERIALS

FIGURE 4.2
Open housing supply system
Source: Based on Turner, 1990

limited range of options for obtaining land, it would be appropriate for the relevant authorities to introduce new ways of bringing land onto the market. This could take many forms, such as:

* taxing undeveloped land at the rate applicable for urbanized land;
* offering tax incentives to developers willing to invest in areas or sectors defined by government policy;
* introducing new forms of land tenure; and
* revising the regulatory framework to remove or relax constraints.

By addressing this issue first, a major improvement can be expected in options for obtaining land. Attention can then be focused on identifying the next constraint, such as options for obtaining credit, etc, until the major constraints have all been addressed. The key issue is that policies need to continually address constraints on the development of more efficient and equitable land and housing markets, in which regulatory frameworks facilitate access to legal housing and urban development rather than inhibit it.

The challenge facing governments is therefore to increase the range of supply options rather than to act as a supplier itself. However, this will only be possible if the regulatory framework permits suppliers to provide what households want and can afford. Since most governments have now agreed to adopt more responsive and appropriate policies, it is more likely that the regulatory framework is a factor.

Once the need to review regulatory frameworks has been accepted, the next issue to address is how to undertake such a review. A number of options can be adopted, although it is vital to adopt a comprehensive approach which relates housing and urban development to their economic, social, cultural and environmental contexts.

In the case of reviewing regulatory frameworks for upgrading existing settlements, the options will be influenced by the ability to involve local residents and organizations. In the case of new developments this will not be possible, although every effort should be made to consult with local communities and NGOs active in the housing and urban development sector on local needs and resources. The sustainable livelihoods (SL) approach provides a useful framework for reviewing and revising regulatory frameworks for upgrading existing urban settlements. In new urban developments the SL approach can also be applied, although an alternative is to undertake a regulatory audit to compare existing guidelines with regulations, standards and procedures actually adopted in informal settlements as a means of comparing the two and identifying key disparities and the reasons for them. This can help to suggest priorities for changing guidelines to reduce such disparities. In practice, the SL and regulatory audit approaches can be used together or separately, depending on conditions and resources.

The choice of methods for collecting and analysing information on regulatory frameworks will be influenced by the technical capabilities of the personnel involved, together with the time, funds and technical facilities available. Where these are abundant, a combination of statistically significant surveys, detailed case studies and other methods will offer a comprehensive and objective basis for decision-making. However, in many cases, it will be necessary to be more flexible and use scarce resources with imagination to obtain a sound and reliable basis for promoting change.

Fortunately, a range of options is available to those responsible for reviewing regulatory frameworks. The main principles involved in selecting the most appropriate methods and tools can be found on the CD-Rom.

USING A SUSTAINABLE LIVELIHOODS (SL) APPROACH

SL is a way of thinking about the objectives, scope and priorities for development in order to enhance progress in poverty reduction. SL

approaches are based on core principles that emphasize people-centred, responsive and multi-level approaches to development (Ashley and Carney, 1999, p45).

The most commonly quoted definition of livelihoods is the following:

> 'A **livelihood** *comprises the capabilities, assets (stores, resources, claims and access) and activities required for a means of living: a livelihood is* **sustainable** *which can cope with and recover from stress and shocks, maintain or enhance its capabilities and assets, and provide* sustainable *livelihood opportunities for the next generation; and which contributes net benefits to other livelihoods at the local and global levels and in the long and short term.'* (Chambers and Conway, 1992, pp7–8, emphasis added).

SL frameworks are diagrammatic tools intended to improve our understanding of livelihoods. They help to illustrate various factors

Meeting members of a community can help in reviewing regulatory frameworks and discussing possible improvements

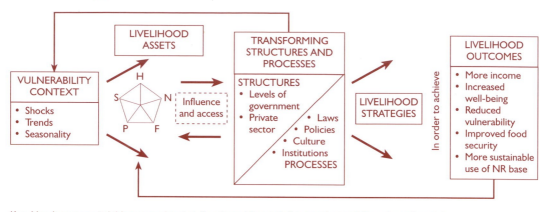

Key: H = human capital; N = natural capital; F = financial capital; S = social capital; P = physical capital

FIGURE 4.3
DFID's sustainable livelihoods framework

Source: Ashley and Carney, 1999, p47

which constrain or enhance livelihood opportunities, and to show how they relate to each other.[1] SL frameworks provide a useful conceptual methodology for understanding the situation of poor people in urban areas, including those living and working in informal settlements.

The SL framework developed by DFID views people pursuing livelihoods in a *vulnerability context*, whereby they are exposed to external shocks and stresses (see Figure 4.3). Within this context they have access to various *livelihood assets* – natural capital, physical capital, human capital, social capital and financial capital (see Box 4.1). *Livelihood strategies* – the ways in which people combine and use assets in pursuit of *livelihood outcomes* – are also influenced by this environment. The viability and effectiveness of livelihood strategies is dependent on the availability and accessibility of assets, which can be positively enhanced or adversely undermined by *policies*, *institutions* and *processes*.

Vulnerability context

The vulnerability context is the external environment (physical, socio-economic and political) in which people live. It includes population trends, resource trends (including conflict), national/international economic trends, trends in governance (including politics), technological trends, human health shocks, natural shocks, economic shocks, conflict, crop/livestock health shocks, and seasonality of prices, production, health and employment opportunities.

Livelihood assets

Livelihood assets include human capital, natural capital, financial capital, social capital and physical capital (see Box 4.1). People may have access to all or just some of these assets. An SL approach seeks to build on the assets to which people have access, as well as their strengths and resourcefulness, rather than emphasizing need and weakness. In order to do this, an understanding of the following is important:

- Levels of assets and their distribution among individuals, households, groups and communities (disaggregating by gender).
- The roles assets play in livelihoods.
- Asset interactions.
- Changes in asset status over time (cycles within a year as well as longer-term changes).
- Constraints on access to assets.

Many of the answers to questions about access to, and use of, assets will be found not through an investigation of the assets themselves, but through an investigation of the relationships between assets and other components of the SL frameworks, including policies, institutions and processes.

Box 4.1 Capital assets

Natural capital: The natural resource stocks from which resources that are useful for livelihoods are derived, eg land, water, biodiversity, environmental resources.

Social capital: The social resources (relationships of trust, membership of groups, networks, access to wider institutions) on which people draw in pursuit of livelihoods.

Human capital: The knowledge, skills, ability to labour, information and good health important to the ability to pursue livelihoods.

Physical capital: The basic infrastructure (water, sanitation, energy, transport, communications), housing and the means and equipment of production.

Financial capital: The financial resources that are available to people (savings, credit, regular remittances or pensions) and which provide them with different livelihood options.

Policies, institutions and processes

The *policies*, *institutions* and *processes* (PIPs) dimension of SL frameworks comprises the institutional and social context within which individuals, households and communities pursue their livelihoods. It is a complex range of issues associated with participation, power, authority, governance, laws, policies, regulations, standards, procedures, public service delivery, social relations (gender, caste, ethnicity), institutions (laws, markets, land tenure arrangements) and organizations (government agencies, NGOs, private sector, civil society organizations).

PIPs influence livelihoods at all levels, from the individual and household to the international and global levels. They operate in all spheres, from the most private to the most public. They influence significantly the conditions that enable or constrain the pursuit of multiple livelihood strategies and the achievement of SL. PIPs determine not only access to the various livelihood assets, but also whether they can be used or transferred, as well as options for livelihood strategies. Some of the structures and processes that affect access to land, infrastructure and housing are presented in Table 4.1.

Livelihood strategies

Livelihood strategies are the full portfolio of livelihood activities that people undertake in order to achieve their livelihood goals (including productive activities, investment strategies, reproductive choices, etc), linked to an understanding of the options and decisions underlying them. Livelihood strategies are dynamic processes in which people combine activities to meet their various needs at different times. Of particular importance in household livelihood strategies are the assets to which households have access and the context in which they operate.

Four categories of livelihood strategies can generally be distinguished:

1 Survival strategies that seek to prevent destitution and death.
2 Coping strategies that seek to minimize the impact of livelihood shocks.
3 Adaptive strategies that seek to spread risk through livelihood adjustment or income diversification.

	Land	Access to: Infrastructure services	Shelter
Structures			
Public sector	• Efficacy of organizations that make and enforce legislation	• Efficacy of organizations that make and enforce legislation	• Efficacy of organizations that make and enforce legislation
Private commercial	• Existence of credit organizations and land traders	• Existence of private sector providers, both formal and informal	• Existence of building organizations, material suppliers, transport and credit organizations
Civil society	• Existence of local resource management organizations	• Existence of self-help, self-build groups	• Existence of self-help, self-build groups
Processes			
Policy	• National land-use policies • Policies on decentralization of resource management	• National land-use policies • Policies on decentralization of infrastructure services • Policies on deregulation	• National land-use policies • Policies on settlement priorities, credit availability, etc
Legislation	• National/local authority land legislation • The rule of law in general (security of people/transactions)	• National/local authority infrastructure legislation • Infrastructure standards	• National/local authority land legislation • The rule of law in general (security of people/ transactions) • Housing, health and social law
Institutions	• Local conventions on land allocation/ inheritance • Informal restrictions on land ownership • Existing ownership rights and power relations • The state of land markets	• Informal restrictions on operation of services • Existing ownership rights and power relations • The level of infrastructure provision	• Local conventions on land allocation/inheritance • Informal restrictions on shelter ownership • Existing ownership rights and power relations • The state of housing/land markets
Culture	• Internal household power relations and conventions on access to land	• Internal household power relations and conventions on access to infrastructure	• Internal household power relations and conventions on access to shelter

4   Accumulation strategies that seek to increase income flows and stocks of assets.

In reality, livelihood strategies are better characterized as a continuum rather than discrete categories (Devereux, 1999).

TABLE 4.1

Types and levels of structures and processes that affect access to land, infra-structure and housing

- WHAT ELSE CAN I DO TO IMPROVE MY RESOURCES?

- WHAT IF I CANNOT DO THIS WORK ANYMORE?

- HOW CAN I GET MORE OUT OF THIS WORK?

- WHAT IF SOMETHING HAPPENS TO ME?

LIVELIHOOD STRATEGY

The key elements of a livelihood strategy

Livelihood outcomes

Livelihood outcomes are the achievements or outputs of livelihood strategies. It should not be assumed that people are solely dedicated to maximizing their income. Rather, they can pursue a range of livelihood outcomes: food security, education for their children, good health and reduced vulnerability are examples. Livelihood outcomes can, in most cases, be thought of as the inverse of poverty. For example, if an individual describes poverty as powerlessness and a lack of access to basic urban services, then the livelihood outcomes he or she seeks might be expected to be empowerment and improved access to services.

Using a sustainable livelihoods approach to analyse the impact of regulatory frameworks on access to livelihood assets[1]

SL frameworks highlight the inter-linkages between livelihoods and regulatory frameworks (see Box 4.2). Understanding such relationships allows the regulatory-making process and the implementation of regulatory measures to be better informed and reoriented to serve the needs and capacities of the urban poor.

Box 4.2 How regulatory frameworks affect access to, and development of, livelihood assets by the urban poor

Natural capital

- *Urban land is a scarce resource.* Because serviced land is in short supply, the poor are frequently unable to access the available plots and end up squatting on marginal land within or on the fringes of towns or cities.
- *The urban environment is under threat.* Although regulatory frameworks to control pollution from industries may exist, they are often poorly enforced and disregarded, sometimes with disastrous consequences in neighbouring informal settlements (eg, the tragic 1984 gas leak incident in Bhopal, India).
- *The environmental agenda may be at odds with the livelihoods of the urban poor.* The increasing influence of the environmental lobby on the sustainable development agenda means that the social and economic dimensions, which arguably impact more directly on those living in poverty, are subordinated.

Physical capital

- *Current standards, regulations and procedures are not affordable to the poor.* In most developing countries, the urban poor majority cannot afford the cost of housing – a vital livelihood asset – that meets existing regulatory requirements.
- *Security of tenure is important to stimulate investment in infrastructure and housing.* Without secure tenure, which is difficult to obtain under existing regulatory frameworks, poor people are at risk of eviction or demolition, and will therefore not invest in infrastructure or housing.
- *Most regulatory frameworks do not favour the incremental development, upgrading or transformation of housing.* Urban poor people who build their own houses typically do so in stages over a protracted period, partly because it is difficult for them to access housing finance, but also sometimes to avoid risks.
- *Regulations and standards often restrict the choice of building materials and technologies that can be used in housing development.* Many specify the use of costly, factory-produced and often imported materials. Alternatives are frequently readily available and widely used in informal settlements, but are not acceptable to regulatory authorities.

Financial capital

- *Regulatory frameworks prevent the poor from engaging in income-generating activities in residential areas.* Most zoning regulations prevent mixed land uses, largely for environmental reasons. But home-based enterprises (HBEs) are the main sources of income for poor people, especially women.

- *Construction of housing and infrastructure can be an important source of income for artisans.* This will, however, be determined largely by what building materials and technologies are permitted by prevailing regulatory frameworks.

Human capital

- *Standards, regulations and procedures do not enable the use of poor people's skills, capacities and potential.* The use of human capital, perhaps the most critical asset that poor people possess, is constrained by regulatory frameworks that do not permit and promote the use of appropriate building materials and technologies.

Social capital

- *Housing development and settlement upgrading can build social capital.* Building and planning regulations, standards and procedures may affect the development of social capital. For instance, stipulating the use of conventional building materials and construction technologies may prevent the use of self-help or mutual aid, which is common in traditional building practices.

Sources: Lowe and Schilderman, 2001; Schilderman and Lowe, 2002 (see CD-Rom)

Livelihoods analysis requires a flexible approach, whereby a range of different methods are employed as appropriate, and a range of stakeholders (identified through stakeholder analysis) are involved. Appropriate research methods and tools for an analysis that covers key aspects of livelihoods are outlined in Table 4.2. Analysis of secondary information (eg participatory poverty assessments, project documents and other existing analyses and reports, web-based material, etc.) is also important. Data produced from livelihood analyses should always be disaggregated (eg by gender, age and socio-economic stratum). The power relationships between different groups of stakeholders should also be taken into account and analysed (see accompanying CD-Rom for more detailed descriptions and advice on different research methods and tools).

The summary findings of a livelihoods analysis of a community in an informal settlement in Colombo, Sri Lanka that had been upgraded are presented in Box 4.3 and on the CD-Rom.

Box 4.3 Summary of the findings of a livelihoods analysis of Siribara Menikepura Urban Upgrading Settlement

Physical

- Each household has 50m^2 land.
- Permanent houses.
- Each household has a pipe-borne water supply.
- Each household has an electricity supply.
- Telephone service is available.
- A vehicular access road (15 feet wide) links with the area road network from three sides of the settlement.
- The settlement is close to services in the area: markets, schools, bus stations, banks, private and government offices, etc.

Social

- CBOs are active in the settlement.
- Community Development Council (CDC).
- Cooperative shop and post office within the settlement.
- Community manages the pre-school and community health centre with the support of Moratuwa Municipal Council.
- Community has strong links with Moratuwa Municipal Council, NGOs, government organizations and CBOs.
- Mixed community with different religions and races.
- Calm and friendly.

Human

- Community includes people with various skills: masons, drivers etc.
- Community leaders.
- Small business enterprise skills.
- Community project management skills.
- Public service operational and management skills.

Financial

- The location of the settlement provides livelihood options for people.
- Employment opportunities are provided by the nearby university (50 per cent of household heads work there).
- There is a small business in front of the university.
- Work is provided by private companies around the settlement (garment industry).
- Three-wheeled vehicles may be hired from stands.
- Small catering services are provided to government officials.

Source:
SEVANATHA–Urban
Resource Centre,
2001

Issues/themes	Methods/tools
Vulnerability context	• Study of meteorological and demographic data • Research in historical archives with a particular focus on political conflict and market fluctuations
Livelihood assets	• Livelihood diagrams • Asset surveys and resource mapping, including soil and vegetation surveys and inventories of the quality of housing stock, water supply and sanitation systems • Seasonal calendars of asset availability and quality • Social network and Venn/chapatti diagrams
Livelihood strategies	• Ranking of income sources • Mapping of migration patterns • Inventory and ranking of income and expenditure • Seasonal calendars of production, employment and income
Livelihood outcomes	• Well-being ranking of social groups, communities or populations in regions (at different moments in recent history) • Social mapping • Cause–effect diagrams • Study of aerial photographs, geographic information systems and remote sensing images and data, with a particular focus on environmental change
PIPs	• Venn/chapatti diagrams • Actor–network analysis and power network diagrams • Cause–effect and flow diagrams • Market analyses • Narratives or institutional histories from key informants (including traditional rules, tenure law and practice and/or markets)

TABLE 4.2
Research methods and tools applicable to a livelihoods approach

Note: Definitions and details of the above tools and methods can be found in the accompanying CD-Rom.

UNDERTAKING A REGULATORY AUDIT FOR IMPROVING ACCESS TO LEGAL SHELTER FOR THE URBAN POOR

What is a regulatory audit?

A regulatory audit is a comprehensive review of regulations, standards and administrative procedures relating to urban land development. It provides a record of all the laws, bylaws, decrees and other official norms that seek to determine what developers, landowners, communities and residents are entitled to do with and on urban land. In their entirety, these various norms constitute the regulatory framework for urban planning and building. Unless specified otherwise, they should apply equally to all groups,

An audit can help to make sense of how the regulatory framework shapes the urban environment and show what can be done to reduce future negative impacts

organizations or individuals seeking to acquire, develop or transfer urban land.

An audit is a comprehensive summary of all planning regulations, standards and administrative procedures to which urban development should conform. It can also:

- compare these official requirements with the standards and procedures by which informal or unauthorized developments take place and indicate the differences between the two; and
- indicate the degree to which an individual regulation, standard or procedure is considered to represent a constraint on accessing legal and affordable shelter by the urban poor.

Why do a regulatory audit?

Regulatory audits can assess the impact of the regulatory framework on land and housing markets. These markets strongly influence the ways in which all sections of the population are able to obtain land, shelter, services and credit. An audit can therefore identify the extent to which the regulatory framework facilitates or constrains such access. It is especially helpful in identifying changes that can improve access to legal housing by the poor and other vulnerable groups, such as women.

Laws, regulations and other official requirements relating to urban land development are usually extremely complicated. In many cases, this is because they have been in place for many years and may even have been inherited from colonial administrations. Subsequent changes may have imposed different requirements without necessarily removing the earlier ones from the statute book. At the same time, requirements may have different levels of official status, in that some may be mandatory and others discretionary. Some may be imposed nationally by central government, and others by provincial or local authorities, many of which may not be applicable consistently.

As if these complications were not enough, the language used may be English or another language not widely understood locally, and the text may be full of terms and phrases only comprehensible to professionals.

For all of these reasons, a regulatory audit can help to clarify what people are expected to do in order to meet official requirements. However, an audit serves a more useful policy objective. It enables those responsible for formulating and implementing the myriad requirements to assess the extent to which changes may be necessary in order to ensure that the regulatory framework is consistent with urban planning and management policy objectives. Requirements based on outdated assumptions or objectives (such as protecting the earlier interests of colonial elites) or inappropriate conditions (such as high levels of economic development) can be removed or revised to reflect current realities and expectations. An audit can highlight those aspects of planning regulations, standards and administrative procedures which can ensure that the regulatory framework facilitates planned development and meets the needs of all sections of the population, not just an affluent minority.

What benefits can a regulatory audit offer?

Regulatory audits provide urban managers with an objective basis for identifying and monitoring individual components of the regulatory framework. Second, they provide civil society groups and others working with the poor with evidence of what changes need to be made to improve access to legal shelter. Third, they can help monitor the impact of regulatory changes in facilitating planned development and reducing the need for squatting and other forms of unauthorized development. They can therefore be key tools in the development of pro-poor urban development strategies.

A key part of the regulatory audit is to establish whether people are aware of and understand the regulatory guidelines that affect them

What are the limitations of a regulatory audit?

As with any audit, the value of a regulatory audit depends largely on the accuracy and level of information available. The methods and tools used to collect and analyse the information are therefore critical. Collecting information on the relevant legislation, planning and building codes is a time-consuming task, although not a difficult one. However, assessing the extent to which a specific component represents a constraint on accessing legal shelter for the poor will require sensitivity and a degree of objectivity which can best be achieved by obtaining the views of those directly involved. This suggests that it is preferable for a local NGO, consultancy or university to be commissioned to undertake the audit. In developing a format for the regulatory audit for this manual, various concepts and definitions, together with ways of assessing degrees of constraint, were considered. The framework finally proposed is a compromise between the need to propose a concrete example which can be used immediately, and a recognition that every situation is unique and changing all the time. While a standardized format is provided in the accompanying CD-Rom, it is important to adapt it to local conditions before undertaking the audit.

How to undertake a regulatory audit

Regulatory audits involve a number of steps, with tasks allocated to each one. These are summarized below.

How to undertake a regulatory audit – step 1

The first step in reviewing the regulatory framework involves listing all existing legislation, bylaws, statutes and other regulations, standards and administrative procedures relating to urban land development and housing. This involves a desk-top review, but may be supplemented by interviews with key stakeholders, including government officials, NGO staff, community organizations, professionals active in the sector, academics and especially low-income residents themselves.

The list of relevant authorities will be important later when discussing possible changes to specific aspects of the regulatory framework (for information and advice on undertaking a stakeholder analysis, see accompanying CD-Rom).

Task 1
1   Decide on the types of information needed for the audit.
2   Decide on the methods to be used for data collection, analysis and recommendations in the audit.
3   Identify the forms of data each method will reveal.
4   Identify the various activities for the study and the way the study is to be conducted.

(For information and advice on how to choose your methods, see accompanying CD-Rom).

Task 2

1 Identify regulatory authorities, the various actors and their key roles at local and national levels.
2 Identify the providers connected with housing including public, semi-public and private agencies.
3 Identify other key stakeholders like NGOs, CBOs, associations, housing federations, political parties etc.

Task 3

1 Build a list of all relevant documentation and legislation to be reviewed.
2 List local planning regulations, standards and procedures.

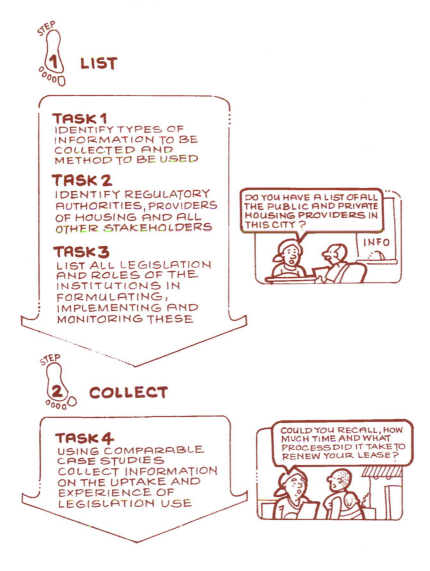

How to undertake a regulatory audit? A summary diagram

4

3   List all the provisions of the regulations related to housing.
4   Identify the role(s) played by each agency in formulating, implementing and monitoring the regulatory framework.

How to undertake a regulatory audit – step 2

The second step involves obtaining information on the existing regulations, standards and administrative procedures followed in typical examples of formal and non-formal urban developments.

Meetings with residents and developers in both formal and non-formal or customary settlements will be needed in order to compare the differences in the standards, regulations and procedures followed and the reasons for the differences. Attention should be focused on identifying the extent to which people are aware of official requirements. In recent research, interviews were held with residents and cards presented which contained both real and some non-existent official regulations or standards in order to identify their levels of awareness. A large proportion of interviewees could not correctly identify the real regulations! In some countries, they are not even well known to the officials responsible for implementing them (Hall, 2004; see also accompanying CD-Rom for report and outline of card sorting exercise).

When completing the administrative procedures section, it is important to note the number of steps involved in each stage of the land registration and development process, and the time taken on average for each. In a landmark study of regulatory frameworks in Peru, the Institute for Liberty and Democracy instructed researchers to follow the procedures required by official agencies as if they were typical applicants. Such an approach may take a considerable time, so asking developers and others involved in submitting proposals through official channels might be easier and quicker. Since international research suggests that administrative procedures are invariably the largest single constraint on accessing legal shelter, especially when inflation and interest rates are high, it is important to be accurate on this point.

It will also be necessary to distinguish between regulations and standards, although this will vary according to local conditions. For example, should an official requirement that densities be within a specific range be considered a regulation or a standard? This is open to local interpretation and the surveys included factors according to where they seemed most relevant, on the understanding that they could be moved if necessary.

Task 4

1   Identify typical formal and informal developments for case studies. To be comparable, developments should have been built at a similar time, in a similar area (comparable land prices) and for target populations with similar incomes.

2   Collect information from residents and developers about what standards, procedures and regulations they are aware of.

3   Talk to all the concerned actors and end-users to find out about any bottlenecks, informal costs, delays, harassment, complexities in the procedures and the number of agencies involved, etc.

4   List the planning regulations, standards and procedures which are actually followed in two case study developments, identifying the formal and informal processes involved. These may include unofficial payments.

5   Identify the number of different steps in the administrative procedure for accessing legal shelter that is undertaken by the end-user. Where possible, have researchers follow the process themselves.

How to undertake a regulatory audit – step 3

When completing the matrix, it is important to balance the factors considered most critical in constraining access to legal shelter (see Table 4.3). However, in each case, the responses by low-income households themselves should be given priority, since these are the groups most directly affected.

It is then recommended that the degree to which each component of the regulatory framework represents a constraint on accessing legal shelter should be assessed. This is not a simple matter of comparing like with like. For example, on what basis can a time delay in processing applications be considered equal to the cost of meeting a specific standard? Responses from a wide range of households on the extent to which a particular factor represents a constraint are to some extent subjective and open to interpretation. This perceptual problem increases when respondents are drawn from a wide range of stakeholders, not just low-income households. For example, professionals may see themselves as responsible for maintaining decent standards of development, while developers may see the same standard as an impediment to affordable legal shelter.

Experience suggests that the best solution to this problem is to obtain the views of residents in both formal and informal

4

developments, since they will be more aware of the differences. However, it will be important to note the extent of any direct or indirect subsidies provided, since this will significantly affect the costs to residents and therefore to governments and society at large.

Task 5

1   Analyse, if possible, the actual or imputed costs associated with meeting legal standards and regulations, and of the administrative procedures that must be followed to do so.

2   Identify the barriers which these standards, regulations and administrative procedures represent from the perspective of those in both formal and informal developments. These may take the form of monetary costs, time demands, numbers of steps, lack of information, lack of contacts, etc.

STEP
3

ANALYSE

TASK 5
UNRAVEL THE REAL IMPACT OF REGULATION ON THE RESOURCES AT THE DISPOSAL OF THE POOR

TASK 6
CATEGORIZE THE REGULATIONS AND ALLOCATE IMPACT ON THE LIVELIHOOD ASSETS OF THE POOR

TASK 7
COMPLETE REGULATORY MATRIX TO CONSOLIDATE THE INFORMATION

TIME SPENT WAITING OUTSIDE AN OFFICE SHOULD BE COUNTED AS WAGES LOST...!!

INTERPRETING REGULATIONS

STEP
4

PRESENTATION
TO STAKEHOLDERS WHO CAN IMPROVE REGULATORY FRAMEWORKS

THE COMPLETED MATRIX SHOWS THAT THERE ARE MANY HURDLES FOR THE POOR TO ACCESS LEGAL SHELTER...

REVIEW OF REGULATION RESULTS

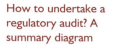

How to undertake a regulatory audit? A summary diagram

3 Assess any gender-specific constraints or barriers, such as women's movements being constrained in public arenas.

Assessing the information collected

Having resolved the methods by which data is collected, the next decision is how to identify the factors to be assessed. The focus of this manual is on planning rather than building or infrastructure issues, although the distinction between them is not always clear. For example, do building setbacks from the front and sides of a plot constitute a building regulation or a planning regulation? Similarly, do infrastructure standards and regulations allow for incremental land development or communal provision? Such distinctions are open to local interpretation and can be seen as impacting on both building design and urban densities. For the purposes of the project, and for regulatory audits, it is perhaps therefore less important how they are classified than that they are listed for consideration. As stated earlier this also applies to the distinction between planning regulations and standards.

To cross-check the assessments of the factors considered to represent constraints, an effective method is to organize a workshop for a wide range of stakeholders, including representatives from the low-income settlements where fieldwork has been conducted (see Box 4.4). This enables cross-checks to be made of the factors considered to represent constraints and will help to validate the findings of the audit. The workshop can also provide a forum in which key stakeholders can consider revisions to the existing regulatory framework.

Box 4.4 Verification workshops

- Policy-makers and implementing agencies should be invited to participate in the verification workshop to bring out the issues related to the draft recommendations, and to encourage commitment to their implementation.
- Other important stakeholders to involve are the people affected by the regulations, such as low-income groups or informal settlement dwellers. This will help verify which changes they feel are most important and will allow policy-makers to hear about the realities the poor face, in their own words.
- The verification workshop helps to build consensus for the draft recommendations based on the assessed constraints.

Note: For information and advice on other available tools and methods, see CD-Rom.

Once the views of all stakeholders have been obtained, the degree to which each regulatory component can be considered a constraint can be indicated provisionally and modified in the light of further assessments by other stakeholders, such as professionals, developers, NGOs and government officials.

In the research which forms the basis of this manual, it was intended to measure or impute an economic cost to each regulation, standard and administrative procedure, so that comparisons between them would be objective. In reality, this is extremely difficult to achieve, since costs for some components are almost impossible to measure. It is therefore recommended that a simple five-point scale be used to indicate the degree to which a specific regulation, standard or procedure is considered to represent a constraint on access to legal shelter.

Task 6

1 Establish criteria for categorizing planning standards and regulations.
2 Organize workshop or focus group discussions with all stakeholders and users represented to verify analysis and generate further insights.
3 Indicate the degree of constraint or cost represented by each standard, regulation or procedure.
4 Develop an analysis of what forms of constraint each represents or what demand each makes on the livelihood assets of the poor.

Presenting the findings of the regulatory audit

The next consideration is how to present the information obtained. This is particularly important for making policy and management decisions. Mayors or other elected representatives responsible for formulating or implementing policies on urban planning need information to be presented in ways that highlight the policy options, rather than dwell in detail on technical aspects, for which they employ professionals. For this reason, it is desirable to present a summary of the information obtained in the form of a matrix listing all the factors under the three headings: planning regulations, planning standards and administrative procedures. These can then be ranked in terms of the degree to which they are considered to represent a constraint on access to legal shelter by the urban poor.

The regulatory matrix proposed in the accompanying CD-Rom presents information on a number of factors under each heading (planning regulations, planning standards and administrative procedures). These include:

- the way in which each component applies in typical formal/statutory and informal/customary settlements;
- the degree to which a particular factor is considered a constraint on access to legal shelter;
- the authority or agency responsible for such factors (in some cases, such as bylaws, these may be under local control, while legal aspects are more likely to be determined by central government); and
- a column for comments – the matrix allows for the addition of factors applicable to local conditions, while some may be deleted if not applicable.

Task 7
Complete the regulatory matrix with the information obtained.

1   First, insert the standards, regulations and procedures which have been shown to exist in case study contexts.
2   Insert the institutions responsible for each of these.
3   Insert the ways these are manifested in both the formal and the informal developments.
4   Indicate the degree to which each factor is considered a constraint on accessing legal housing.
5   In the comments section, include specific issues – such as gender variations – which have emerged.

As with any new approach, it will take experience to assess the most critical factors for which change is needed. This should not be used as an excuse for not making a start, although civil servants will need the confidence and support of their superiors if it requires them to take what they consider to be avoidable risks. It may be advisable to initiate the process of change modestly in order to win confidence and build experience.

Regulatory element		Responsible authority for policy and implementation	Formal/ statutory norm	
PLANNING REGULATIONS				
Setbacks (increase with height of buildings)	Minimum front margin if pathway	Local authority by way of development control regulations, approved by the state government. Provided by architects and verified by building permission department	1.0m	
	Minimum front margin if road		1.5m	
	Minimum rear margin if detached		1.5m	
Building heights	Maximum height of building if single storey		4.0m	
Ground coverage	Maximum construction on ground		No restriction for residential buildings	
Plot and building use	Restriction on plot use		Restricted to residential unless otherwise permitted	
	Land-use controls/zoning		Compatible uses permitted in each zone	
	Rental/ subletting	Government of India, no-one pays	If rented, income tax is to be paid	
	Economic activity	CIDCO can permit other compatible non-residential land uses under a policy called 'expansion of user' by charging additionally	Compatible uses with prior permission and payment	
etc...				
PLANNING STANDARDS – see India case study on CD-Rom for more details				
Plot level for plotted development	Minimum plot area	Local authority by way of development control regulations, approved by the state government. Provided by planning and verified by building permission departments	25 sq m	
etc...				
ADMINISTRATIVE PROCEDURES – see India case study on CD-Rom for more details				
etc...				

TABLE 4.3

Regulatory matrix with selected inputs for regulatory elements in Navi Mumbai, India

Source: Adusumilli and Shekdar, 2004

Informal/ customary norm	Degree of constraint					Remarks
	1	2	3	4	5	
0m	x					The front margins can go. Rear margins needed as service cores. Slums have rear service lane as a public space, hence zero rear margin required for plots
0m	x					
0m (see Remarks)						
4.0m	x	x	x	x	x	In single storey housing, the poor want higher roofs to provide a mezzanine floor
100% of plot area covered by construction						Setbacks govern this
As per demand	x	x	x			Regional parks constitute a land-use category in which residential use is not permissible. Regularization of encroachments can be done only with statutory modification of land-use which is time-consuming
Regional Parks Zone	x	x	x			
Yes						
15% shops	x	x	x			

18 sq m						Any changes in these regulations are generally brought about by special government schemes to make them economical. However, the minimum plot size was increased from 21 sq m to 25 sq m in 1992

5 GUIDING PRINCIPLES FOR EFFECTING CHANGE

Developing regulatory frameworks should be a participatory and continuous process

If regulatory frameworks are to enable poor people living and working in informal settlements to gain access to assets that are vital to the achievement of sustainable livelihoods (SL), or to enable urban poor households to gain access to affordable new housing, there are certain principles to which they must adhere. While compliance to these principles will not necessarily ensure success, non-compliance will guarantee failure. These principles require that all stakeholders involved in urban development should:

RECOGNIZE AND ACCEPT REALITIES ON THE GROUND

Development agencies should recognize and understand the realities on the ground and the contribution of households living in poverty to the urban economy.

All key stakeholders in urban upgrading and new housing development must be engaged if regulatory change is to be effective (see Box 5.1). Collaboration between central and local authorities, communities, private sector developers, professionals, finance institutions and development agencies is the best way to meet existing and future shelter needs. Although market forces may prove dominant, there is considerable scope to influence, guide and regulate their impact through innovative, flexible partnerships.

Regular dialogue and gender-sensitive participation of the various stakeholders involved in urban upgrading and new housing development at all levels and stages of decision-making should be facilitated. This includes maximizing dialogue between all stakeholders to review, revise and develop, where necessary, regulatory frameworks to improve livelihoods and living conditions for all, especially the poor.

FOCUS ON KEY ASPECTS OF PUBLIC CONCERN

Regulatory frameworks should be relevant, realistic and in the public interest.

Regulations should be simple, easily accessible and understood by all stakeholders. They should also focus on those aspects which protect the public interest but allow residents maximum local

control. To avoid excessive regulation, realistic targets should be set and mechanisms put in place that rely as much as possible on self-regulation. The differentiation between self-regulation and external regulation, with closer inspection of the nuances of the regulatory framework, should be given more importance (see Box 5.2).

Housing that is designed without due consideration for the needs of the people often fails to attract any takers

UNDERSTAND AND ACKNOWLEDGE THE KNOWLEDGE AND INFORMATION SYSTEMS OF PEOPLE LIVING IN POVERTY

The sharing of knowledge, information and experience should be promoted, especially at the grass-roots level, between communities.

Organizations of the urban poor are an important source of innovation and action at the local level and have a strong interest and proven ability to promote sustainable livelihoods. Poor communities have used knowledge and information that they themselves have generated to challenge the inadequate and

5

Box 5.1 Achieving participatory change in Sri Lanka

In Sri Lanka, urban local authorities (ULAs) have the power to prepare planning regulations and standards with community participation under the Planning and Building Regulations Law gazetted in 1986. Formal planning regulations and standards are not applicable in special project areas under the UDA Law. It has been possible to implement this law in many ULA areas in Sri Lanka for a number of reasons, including the following:

- A policy paper on urban upgrading was approved by the Ministry of Housing and Local Government in 1979. This paper recognized urban upgrading as a key approach for improving the livelihoods of low-income people in urban areas.
- Government programmes to assist the formation and strengthening of CBOs in slums and informal settlements.
- Introduction of a participatory methodology for the development of minimum standards for urban upgrading. Community action planning (CAP) is the methodology used in Sri Lanka for the development of standards for urban upgrading. CAP consists of a series of community workshops held at settlement level for key stakeholders in urban development to interact with the community and decide planning standards that satisfy the needs of the people in slums and shanty towns.
- Implementation of pilot urban upgrading projects using minimum standards developed at community workshops.
- Development of regulatory guidelines for land subdivisions, plot allocation, house building, infrastructure provision and development of community-based enterprises based on the CAP approach.
- Creation of an institutional structure at local authority level to support the design and implementation of community planning and building guidelines. Housing and Community Development Committees at the municipality level have been established to provide policy guidance and monitor urban livelihood programmes, including urban upgrading.

Source: Jayaratne et al, 2003 (see CD-Rom)

inaccurate information that the state uses for reallocating resources for the poor in cities, and have thus been able to use knowledge as an asset for negotiation (see Box 5.3).

Box 5.2 Self-regulation and the formal regulatory framework

The primary concern of regulatory guidelines should be to ensure public health and safety. Anything more than this should be considered optional, especially given the limited technical and human resources available to most urban development and management agencies. The present tendency is for local authorities to try and control everything, with the predictable result that, in practice, they control very little of anything. By concentrating on the basics, public sector influence over new development and the improvement of existing urban areas would be easier to achieve on a sustainable basis.

For matters which primarily affect the residents of a plot, or their immediate neighbours, it should be possible for self-regulation within the community to resolve such problems, whether these relate to land use, building design, construction, etc. For example, in the informal areas of Ankara, Turkey, anyone carrying out development that was considered inappropriate by neighbouring residents could be reported to the municipality. An inspector would then visit and consider the complaints in the light of official regulations and had the authority to enforce or relax the regulations according to his perception of how justified the complaints were. Such flexibility placed the community in the driving seat as far as regulatory guidelines were concerned and reduced pressure on the municipality to a level which it was able to sustain.

Source: Payne, 2001, p9 (see CD-Rom)

ADOPT AN ENABLING ROLE

Governments, both national and local, should support the removal of regulatory barriers and the streamlining of regulatory frameworks to contribute to an enabling environment for urban upgrading and affordable new legal shelter.

The Istanbul Declaration and the Habitat Agenda (UNCHS, 1997) adopted by 171 governments committed them to innovative ways of working to improve the urban environment. This included adopting the role of enabler and developing their capacity to fulfil a pro-poor strategy and guarantee human rights. In situations where the necessary supportive policies, institutions and processes have not been implemented, governments must at least indicate that they are supportive of urban upgrading and affordable shelter for the poor.

5

Source: McLeod, 2003, p4 (see CD-Rom)

INVEST IN PRECEDENTS

Precedents and pilot projects are an effective way of demonstrating, albeit on a small scale, the implications of regulatory change.

Effecting changes to regulatory frameworks will require considerable investment in terms of time, and in the form of precedent setting and pilot projects to convince central and local government authorities and other stakeholders of the importance and benefits of proposed changes. Those with regulatory responsibility are commonly very resistant to change, and therefore have to be thoroughly convinced: for many, seeing is believing (see Box 5.4).

Effecting change in regulatory frameworks may require investment in pilot projects to establish good practice and to convince central and local government authorities and other stakeholders of the importance and benefits of proposed changes

Box 5.4 Precedents for planning and building standards

'In 1987, pavement women in Mumbai who had formed a collective organisation known as Mahila Milan, began to dream about the housing they wanted to live in. They constructed cardboard house models and later full size models, inviting professionals and officials to come and discuss the designs that they had created. One of the important features of the models that they eventually judged to be both acceptable and affordable, was a 14ft back wall with a sloping roof. This feature allowed for the construction of a mezzanine (or loft), nearly doubling the available living space for only a 30 per cent increase in the cost. The problem with this pragmatic idea was that it did not meet local building bylaws which limited ceiling height to 9ft. Burra and Patel have described how this design innovation by pavement dwellers has been tried and tested over time in a variety of different upgrading scenarios including the high rise construction of Rajiv Indira-Suryodaya... However at each stage there has been a battle with officials. The 14ft wall was eventually officially sanctioned after 4 years of lobbying, a process that required prolonged, determined and persistent effort by the Federations and Mahila Milan as well as considerable financial resources to produce practical demonstration models. Without this coordinated action by an organisation representing large numbers of people, it is unlikely that the changes would have been accepted.'

Source: McLeod, 2003
(see CD-Rom)

STRENGTHEN INCLUSIVENESS

City governments should respond to, and be accountable to, all urban residents, including those living in poverty.

Good governance rests on the twin values of inclusiveness and accountability (see Box 5.5). Good urban governance, based on the principle of urban citizenship, affirms that no woman, man or child should be denied access to the necessities of urban life, including adequate shelter, security of tenure, safe water, sanitation, a clean environment, employment and public safety. Regulatory frameworks affect access to all of these. Inclusive decision-making processes and regulatory frameworks should thus be promoted as practical strategies for translating the norms of good urban governance to meet the messy reality of competing interests and priorities, as articulated in the UN-Habitat Global Campaign on Urban Governance (UN-Habitat, 2002). The most powerful antidote to weak accountability is to give citizens a stronger voice, which can help ensure both that public officials pay attention to the quality

> **Box 5.5 Analysing Coastal Regulation Zones in the context of the urban poor**
>
> The alliance of the Society for the Development of Area-based Resources, the National Federation of Slum Dwellers and Mahila Milan (SPARC/NSDF/MM) believes that if regulations have been formulated from narrow class perspectives and only work for a privileged few rather than the population at large, they are essentially undemocratic. The important questions are: how does one assess Coastal Regulation Zone rules in the context of the needs and conditions of the urban poor? Moreover, if these regulations negatively affect the poor, what can be done to change this situation, keeping in mind the importance of protecting the environment? And, lastly, who should judge whether norms, standards and regulations work for the poor in practice?
>
> All these questions strike at the heart of a critical issue: the state's accountability towards its urban poor population.

Source: Burra, 2003, p13 (see CD-Rom)

and coverage of government services, and that citizens' needs are met (Humphreys and Banerji, 2003).

If people living and working in informal settlements are to be able to improve their livelihoods, and they are to be integrated physically and socially into their urban surroundings, discriminatory and exclusionary regulatory requirements must be eliminated. This applies equally to enabling poor households to gain access to legal and affordable new urban housing developments. An inclusive regulatory environment can greatly assist the achievement of sustainable urban upgrading and new urban housing development objectives.

PROMOTE PARTNERSHIPS BETWEEN KEY STAKEHOLDERS

Partnerships between key stakeholders that ensure inclusiveness should be forged and sustained.

Active and effective partnerships are a prerequisite for the success of urban upgrading and new housing development aimed at the poor. Appropriate frameworks, and institutional support that facilitates participation and partnership arrangements at all levels should be established and adopted. A key lesson from international experience is that upgrading is most effective when led by the

Box 5.6 Options for municipal action

Municipalities may review the regulatory framework to ensure that all levels of government, professional departments, politicians and officials will interact, coordinate and build effective alliances with communities and community organizations. Policy-makers need to understand the relative power of groups and organizations, so as to selectively intervene, support and develop meaningful intervention strategies. Municipal authorities should have frequent meetings with CBOs to identify their needs and to disseminate policies addressing poverty in such a way that these policies become internalized by the CBO members. This is a condition for their effective participation.

Source:
Vanderschueren et al,
1996, p14

municipal authority and implemented at the community level through a broad set of intermediaries including CBOs, NGOs, the private sector, and multilateral and bilateral agencies (see Box 5.6). For new development, partnerships between landowners, developers, urban development agencies and NGOs can reduce costs and improve the acceptability of plans.

FACILITATE LOCAL OWNERSHIP OF PROCESSES

Urban poor communities should have an active stake in urban development processes.

Communities need to feel that they are active partners in the development process if they are to realize their potentials and take ownership of processes and interventions that will impact on their livelihoods. If managed effectively, participation can enhance local ownership of processes and facilities, and contribute to the sustainability of upgrading and new development programmes (see Box 5.7).

IDENTIFY 'CHAMPIONS OF CHANGE' AND CREATE A CRITICAL MASS

'Champions of change' should be identified, as they can be instrumental in creating a critical mass and stimulating regulatory change.

Box 5.7 Increasing community ownership of resettlement processes in India

'The alliance of SPARC/NSDF/MM entered into an agreement with the Government of Maharashtra (GOM) and the Indian Railways (IR) to relocate 900 families... The GOM gave a piece of land at a place called Kanjur Marg and the Indian Railways was to provide funds for infrastructure. The alliance was entrusted with the task of facilitating the resettlement by organizing the community, providing access to housing finance, building the houses and shifting the people... [It] showed a new way of doing things: government provided land, the Railways paid for infrastructure and people took loans to build their own houses. A realignment and renegotiation of roles and relationships between government and NGOs and CBOS took place in which government became a facilitator rather than a provider and a far more proactive role was played by the community in selecting land, designing and helping to construct the houses and moving to the new site on their own... Well-established norms and standards were set aside and new paradigms came up in their place.'

Source: Burra and Patel, 2001 (see CD-Rom)

Regulatory reform can be stimulated by identifying and supporting 'champions of change' (including NGOs, CBOs, reform-minded politicians, civil servants and municipal officials, the media, the private sector, professional associations and the research community). A dual approach is needed which promotes the broader processes of pro-poor regulatory reform and supports champions of change. This includes the creation of a critical mass of support for reform from fragmented stakeholders, and ways of addressing vested interests. Forming a critical mass is essential not only to effect real change, but also to ensure the continuity of initiatives.

In the case of upgrading existing settlements, tools exist for poor communities to generate the required critical mass. They are emerging gradually from research and practical application, and many are already being actively used.[1] Also, there now exists a set of precedents: a protocol. In the case of new urban development, champions of change can be NGO staff, professionals or private sector developers involved in urban development, although the prospect of votes by poor households may encourage local politicians to adopt pro-poor approaches. The important point is that champions may come from anywhere and for any reason, but all deserve support.

APPLY RULES CONSISTENTLY

There should be no favouritism or discrimination in the enforcement of regulatory requirements.

In many countries, regulatory requirements are not enforced with equal rigour in rich and poor areas. The latter usually get the sharp end of the stick, in particular with respect to regulations and standards controlling access to land, infrastructure and housing. If the poor are to be expected to conform to the law, they need to be treated on equal terms with other citizens.

INTEGRATE PLANNING AND DEVELOPMENT STRATEGIES

An agreed strategic framework is needed to meet existing and projected future needs for land, housing and infrastructure.

An integrated, interdisciplinary approach involving different levels of government, NGOs, local communities, landowners and developers is essential to improve the economic and social aspects of urban upgrading and new development. Implementation processes should be streamlined to improve decision-making, internal functioning and community participation.

Cities that plan their moves over decades can expect to waste fewer resources on catching up with rapid growth and poorly-sited services and facilities. Many cities have demonstrated that well-

Champions of change are often people who influence change by leading and guiding people in the correct direction. People often benefit from the skill and knowledge of such people, who can demystify and explain the regulations process

managed growth can extend services to urban poor populations in a way that allows upgrading to higher standards of service in accordance with public and private capacity to pay (Cities Alliance, 2000). Similarly, it is far less expensive to plan new developments than to upgrade existing ones. Developing new areas at initially modest levels of development can dramatically reduce the need for future slums and for the need to upgrade projects in the future.

ACCEPT REGULATION AS A PROCESS RATHER THAN A PRODUCT

Change from traditional regulatory paradigms by framing regulation as a process.

Regulation can be seen in a number of ways. It can be conceived of as a rule or order of conduct prescribed by an authority, either requiring or prohibiting certain behaviour, for various purposes (eg health, safety or environmental objectives). Or it can be looked on as a process or activity in which an authority requires or proscribes certain activities or behaviour on the part of individuals, communities, organizations or institutions, through a continuing administrative process that typically involves specially designated regulatory agencies. Ongoing and constant regulation should expand and increase the value added to the livelihood activities that urban poor people engage in. A continuous revision process should also create and maintain an enabling regulatory framework.

ACKNOWLEDGE THE PRINCIPLE OF INCREMENTAL DEVELOPMENT

'A journey of a thousand miles begins with a single step' – Confucius.

International experience demonstrates that most poor people wish to acquire decent, safe and comfortable housing. Their poverty simply prevents them from achieving this quickly or in a single step. Those that succeed invariably do so by phasing investments when and as resources are available (see Box 5.8). Accepting this incremental approach and incorporating it into the regulatory framework will make it easier for households to enter the legal

The providers and regulators of urban development and housing should aim for a shared understanding of the process of incremental development. This will enable all stakeholders to develop more appropriate regulatory guidelines

housing market and reduce the need for future slums and unauthorized settlements.

GUARANTEE ACCESS TO INFORMATION

Urban poor communities should have ready access to information.

Information is essential if developers and communities are to conform to the terms and conditions of the regulatory framework. It can help reduce uncertainty and vulnerability, as well as enable them to take the initiative in times of crisis. Information should therefore be readily accessible in a language and format that all social groups can understand. This is not the case with most regulatory texts such as planning, building, environmental, fiscal, work, and health and safety documents.

Knowledge and information generated by development agencies and through research which is intended for urban poor communities often ends up in the hands of information brokers (such as NGOs, local chiefs etc), many of whom are not well connected to the target

Box 5.8 Incremental housing development

[A]lmost all locally controlled development is incremental in nature, with people building a modest house initially, which they expand and improve as resources become available. In many cases, such housing reaches official standards eventually, although attempts to impose such standards at the outset raise the bottom rung of the housing ladder too high and exclude people from participating in the legal housing market. Ironically, therefore, standards designed to ensure good-quality urban development are partly responsible for the growth of [unauthorized] and substandard development.

Source: Payne, 2002b, p253

communities or share information selectively. Indeed, this is one of the main reasons why knowledge resulting from research and development programmes has less impact than expected at the grass-roots level. Brokers who do not operate openly should be excluded. However, those who perform well should be helped to produce appropriate information resources in formats that are easily accessible and understood by the urban poor (Schilderman, 2002).

TAKE ADVANTAGE OF WINDOWS OF OPPORTUNITY

Proponents of regulatory reform should be quick to recognize opportunities and make the most of them.

Advocates of pro-poor regulatory change must be ready and able to take advantage of windows of opportunity when they open up. A new government or policy, or an unexpected event, may provide an opportunity to introduce major changes in urban management practice, and those responsible for planning regulations standards and procedures need to be able to respond quickly and positively before the window closes (see Box 5.9). Such changes may arise for many reasons and are difficult to anticipate. Those concerned with ensuring that regulatory frameworks are responsive to the needs and circumstances of the poor need to be alert for any opportunity that arises. Progress may initially be slow, but when change happens, the benefits can be substantial.

Although it is important to take advantage of windows of opportunity, rapid change can generate problems for further reform. Important steps in planning for implementation include identifying the potential obstacles to change, preparing guidelines to support

Box 5.9 Pre-testing of the land allocation domain: the case of Canaan settlement, Mavoko

In the course of implementing the Regulatory Guidelines for Upgrading project, Mavoko Municipal Council was involved in the relocation of over 348 community members from Sinai (which had burnt down) to a settlement called Canaan. The relocation was necessitated by the fact that the community was squatting on private land, which made reconstruction on the old site objectionable. The project took this as an opportunity to pilot the implementation of the revised guidelines on land allocation, in particular, recommendations that: (a) the beneficiaries should be the poor; (b) allottees should be identified using a participatory process; and (c) allotment should be achieved through balloting to ensure equity.

As the upgrading of existing settlements often involves the displacement and relocation of residents, this was an ideal opportunity to demonstrate the implications of the revised guidelines on land allocation procedures. The relocation also presented an opportunity to test the recommended reduced minimum plot sizes. By adopting the reduced plot sizes, it was possible to accommodate a much higher number of households on the new site. This, in turn, presented an opportunity to influence the minimum plot sizes in the Physical Planning Handbook that was being revised by the Ministry of Lands and Settlement at the time.

Source: ITDG–EA, 2003 (see CD-Rom)

change, and identifying the capacity needed to implement change. The gradual implementation of reforms can also allow some details of regulatory design to be determined through experience. Major reforms may need to be broken down into phases or stages to enable their implementation, particularly where they involve establishing new institutions. Such stages also need to be planned with care. It is important to prioritize changes rather than tackle everything at once.

BUILD INSTITUTIONAL CAPACITY

Adequate institutional capacity is required to achieve and sustain regulatory reform.

The envisaged participatory regulatory reform process will place great demands on urban management institutions. Capacity-building and institutional development strategies will thus need to form integral parts of the change process at all levels. To facilitate capacity-building and institutional development for urban upgrading, governments at the appropriate levels, including local authorities and their associations (eg, the Association of Local Government Authorities of Kenya), will have to develop information systems for networking, accessing resources and the exchange, transfer and sharing of experience, expertise, know-how and technology in urban upgrading. They should also ensure that the regulatory framework reflects the needs and resources of the poor and provides institutional support for facilitating participation and partnership arrangements (UNCHS, 1997).

POLITICAL WILL

Pro-poor regulatory reform will be almost impossible to achieve if political will is lacking.

The most important element in implementing pro-poor regulatory reform is, without doubt, political will. If this is lacking, initiatives to upgrade informal settlements and improve access to affordable new shelter are virtually impossible. Political commitment is also crucial for the effective involvement of poor people and housing providers in regulatory reform. Political will is essential at every level, from the national to the local, for implementing successful partnerships and for scaling-up successful interventions. By publicizing research findings, particularly in the popular media, political will can be increased, especially in cases where the research demonstrates that reforms are required and can be achieved relatively easily.

PROFESSIONAL WILL

Professionals need to be convinced of the need for change and aware of the options for achieving it.

While political will is essential in reviewing and implementing changes to the regulatory framework, little progress will be made without the active support of professionals within urban development agencies. Planners, architects, engineers, surveyors and so on are trained to regard themselves as upholding what they consider to be minimum acceptable standards in developing or upgrading urban areas. However, if these prove to be inconsistent with what the poor need or can afford, it is essential that they are willing to compromise on aspects not essential to the wider public interest and that they adapt the regulatory framework so that the poor can conform.

A good example of this is the widespread practice in low-income settlements of incremental development, whereby households improve their dwellings as and when resources are available. It may take them one or two decades to achieve an officially acceptable form of housing following this approach, but there is no reason why it should not be accommodated within planning regulations providing that the key principles of public health and safety are respected. This may require professionals to change the habits and working practices of a lifetime, but it is the only realistic way for planned urban development to be accessible to the poor.

ENFORCEMENT

Regulatory frameworks must be enforced if they are to achieve the desired results.

A key challenge with respect to regulatory requirements is how to enact and enforce them. In many cases, poor people do not respect or adhere to them as they encumber livelihood strategies and access to vital livelihood assets. Such rules may enjoy legality but may lack social legitimacy. Regulatory frameworks should enable access to livelihood assets, as well as facilitate mixed land use and greater control over plot development, providing that public health and safety can be assured. Delegating control to the lowest possible level consistent with these objectives is likely to result in wider implementation if regulatory frameworks are themselves realistic.

EFFECTIVE
REGULATORY
FRAMEWORKS
☐
KEY
PRINCIPLES

··· KEY PRINCIPLES ····

- ☐ RECOGNISE AND ACCEPT GROUND REALITIES.
- ☐ FOCUS ON KEY PUBLIC ISSUES
- ☐ UNDERSTAND INFORMATION SYSTEMS OF PEOPLE IN POVERTY
- ☐ ADOPT AN ENABLING ROLE
- ☐ INVEST IN PRECEDENTS
- ☐ EXTRAPOLATE FROM PILOT PROJECTS
- ☐ STRENGTHEN INCLUSIVENESS
- ☐ PROMOTE PARTNERSHIPS BETWEEN STAKEHOLDERS
- ☐ FACILITATE LOCAL OWNER -SHIP OF PROCESSES
- ☐ IDENTIFY CHAMPIONS OF CHANGE
- ☐ APPLY RULES CONSISTENTLY
- ☐ INTEGRATE PLANNING AND DEVELOPMENT STRATEGIES
- ☐ REGULATION IS A PROCESS
- ☐ ACKNOWLEDGE PRINCIPLE OF INCREMENTAL GROWTH
- ☐ GUARANTEE ACCESS TO INFORMATION
- ☐ TAKE ADVANTAGE OF WINDOWS OF OPPORTUNITY
- ☐ BUILD INSTITUTIONAL CAPACITY
- ☐ ENCOURAGE POLITICAL WILL
- ☐ PROFESSIONAL WILL
- ☐ ENFORCEMENT

Summary of key
principles for effective
regulatory
frameworks

6 SOME FINAL SUGGESTIONS

This manual has tried to demonstrate that regulatory guidelines as widely applied in urban upgrading and new development make it difficult for the poor to obtain or improve legally approved housing. Even many middle-income households find it increasingly difficult to conform to official norms. All the international progress of recent decades in the area of housing policy has not so far yielded significant improvements on the ground. There is therefore a real risk that unless urgent action is taken to identify and remove the constraints on progress, UN forecasts of 1.5 billion people living in urban slums and squatter settlements by 2015 could become a real possibility. Even more worrying is that this number could swell to 2 billion, or *more than double* the present population of slums and squatter settlements by 2030. In other words, if we consider the present situation in towns and cities of the developing world to be worrying, it will become more than twice as bad in less than three decades unless urgent and appropriate action is taken.

The research on which this manual is based has clearly demonstrated that regulatory frameworks are one of, if not *the* major, constraint on reducing the present slum populations and reducing the need for their future growth. We hope that the arguments advanced in support of this view are sufficient to convince politicians, policy-makers, professionals and civil society groups to review existing planning regulations, standards and administrative procedures to see where changes can be made. The aim is not to suggest that standards should be reduced, but that these groups recognize the need for them to be based on economic realities.

The manual also demonstrates that research can generate practical benefits for government agencies responsible for urban management and particularly for the poor themselves. As Box 6.1 shows, even during the short period of the research project on which this manual is based, several countries have implemented some of the recommendations arising from reviews of their regulatory frameworks, and other recommendations are being actively considered.

Box 6.1 Progress in implementing recommendations in selected case study countries

Lesotho

A number of the project recommendations have been incorporated into the draft bill for the new Land Act, although it is not claimed that this is solely the result of this project. The draft bill, which is indicative of current government thinking but may be modified before being approved, proposes the following:

- The vast majority of peri-urban residents who had obtained land through customary practices which were considered illegal will be incorporated into the legal system, providing that they were occupying land 'peaceably, openly and uninterruptedly for a period of not less than three years'.

- Households requiring land purely for residential purposes should be able to obtain a 'primary release' from local authorities at virtually no cost, without being required to have their land surveyed, nor having to travel to the capital to visit half-a-dozen different offices. The case study highlighted the time required and the prohibitive costs involved in the 13 steps necessary to obtain land and housing legally. Only those requiring large tracts of land or using land for non-residential purposes will have to follow more complex procedures.

- '… [T]he Minister shall be responsible for policy formulation and for ensuring the execution *by officials in the Ministry* of such functions connected with the implementation of policies', in line with the study team's recommendation that the Minister and/or Commissioner of Lands no longer be required to approve all land grants in the country.

Bolivia

The Municipal Ordinance has been changed to incorporate several key recommendations of the research, after a senior official affirmed at a project workshop that 'introducing changes in the currently prevailing municipal norms is possible'. The changes, which reflect an acceptance of the need to incorporate traditional ways of defining and using space in informal settlements within the regulatory framework, include the following:

- A reduction in the minimum plot area from 180m^2 to 120m^2 for plots located in the internal part of a block, and to 180m^2 for corner plots, and in the frontage from 8m to 6m, which has enabled densification and a lowering of water and sewerage connection costs.

Note: For all reports on case study countries, see CD-Rom

- Permitting residents to build on 50 per cent of the frontage strip, thereby making it possible to perform economic activities within the home.
- A removal of existing restrictions on construction on rear setbacks and allowing dwellers to build two floors.

Tanzania

Despite generally poor acceptance of research recommendations by a Steering Committee formed to facilitate the achievement of modest changes to the regulatory framework, an opportunity was taken to influence the ongoing review of the Town and Country Planning Ordinance of 1956 during the course of the research project. Changes that have been accepted include the following:

- Decentralization of many land-management powers from the Ministry of Lands.
- Acceptance of flexible planning standards developed and approved at local or regional levels.
- Allowing landowners to prepare their own land-use plans and to have these plans, which will supersede those of planning authorities, approved by the planning authorities.
- A more active role for CBOs and NGOs.

Kenya

- Mavoko Municipal Council is testing the regulatory guidelines proposed by the research.
- Access to municipal offices, departments and services has been made easier, and local community members are now able to attend Town Planning Council meetings.
- Research recommendations on pro-poor land allocation procedures and smaller minimum plot sizes were followed in the relocation of informal settlers to a new site.
- Community-initiated and -managed water points have been constructed in one settlement, and Mavoko Municipal Council is now willing to provide services to informal settlements and allow payment of connection fees in instalments.
- The Department of Physical Planning in the Ministry of Lands and Settlements will now recognize informal settlements in its planning process, maps and diagrams, and has also revised the minimum plot size in urban centres from $110m^2$ to $75m^2$.

Sri Lanka

- An agreement was reached to form a working committee involving the key stakeholders: National Housing Development Authority, Urban Development Authority, Colombo Municipal Council, the Urban Settlement Improvement Programme, SEVANATHA and others. This committee will carry forward the implementation of upgrading projects using the guidelines developed under the Regulatory Guidelines for Urban Upgrading project.
- The Director of the Urban Settlement Improvement Programme has indicated that the proposed regulatory guidelines will be adopted for ongoing upgrading projects under its authority.

India

- Following intensive lobbying by SPARC, the Coastal Zone Management Plan (CZMP) Authority for Maharashtra has agreed to revise the width of the Coastal Regulation Zone-affected area along Mahim creek on the Dharavi side. SPARC's research had revealed this to have been erroneously demarcated as 100m instead of the actual width of the creek.

Note: For all reports on case study countries, see CD-Rom

Opportunities for implementing new approaches will vary from time to time and place to place, but it is important to have options available when the opportunity arises. This is what the manual seeks to provide.

The critical feature of an appropriate regulatory framework is that it defines and protects the public interest without imposing terms and conditions which are of no relevance to the wider community. This is clearly a difficult balance to strike, but a strong case can be made for focusing on key issues of public health and safety rather than seeking to impose terms and conditions which do not enjoy popular acceptance and are costly to conform to, financially or otherwise. Since the poor seek to reduce the initial costs of housing and defer expenditure on improvements and expansions until resources are available, regulatory guidelines can help them in this process by accepting the principle of incremental development.

Of all the ways in which regulatory guidelines can be improved, the research suggests that, in many cases, priority should be given to simplifying the administrative procedures involved in legally accessing urban land and registering, developing or improving a residential plot. Where procedures delay investments, increase risks, or both, they will add to total costs and deter the poor from conforming. This issue is particularly relevant when interest rates, and therefore the cost of borrowing, are high.

Inevitably, this will involve tackling the groups who benefit from the status quo. However, change need not necessarily be to their disadvantage. For example, if officials are given financial incentives for processing increased numbers of applications, and therefore providing better value to applicants, the need to extract benefits from a small number of applicants can be reduced. Should such concessions be insufficient to improve administrative efficiency, then more radical measures, such as outsourcing or privatizing some functions of public administration, might be necessary. These approaches have produced substantial improvements and cost savings in many countries. Similarly, the increasing application of information technology opens up dramatic opportunities to streamline administrative procedures and improve the service given to citizens at affordable costs.

Some hard choices therefore lie ahead for central and local government agencies responsible for urban management and housing. Unless they grasp the need to change, it can confidently be predicted that towns and cities will become even less manageable than they are at present. It is not a prospect that many would welcome. While there may not be many votes in regulatory frameworks, it is likely that the prospect of being able to obtain legal and affordable shelter or improve one's existing housing is something that would win widespread support.

In conclusion, it should be remembered that regulation alone cannot ensure that towns and cities will be pleasant, attractive and stimulating places in which to live, work and play. Regulatory guidelines are essentially a means of seeking to ensure a minimum standard and form of urban development. They cannot therefore act as a substitute for vision and creativity in building urban environments which facilitate rather than constrain, and enhance rather than depress. The quality of the urban environment is determined to a large extent by the layout and use of public space rather than built form, and this is not something which is effectively controlled by current regulations, standards or procedures.

The way people perceive and use space varies to some extent from one culture to another, and every opportunity should be taken in revising regulatory frameworks to enable local traditions in built form and spatial organization to be realized. Under conditions of major social and economic change, such characteristics can provide a valuable sense of continuity and identity. Experience has demonstrated that this can best be achieved through a multidisciplinary approach which includes the active participation of local people.

The methods for reviewing existing regulatory guidelines presented in this manual will hopefully enable readers to identify options for short- and medium-term changes, and increase the ability of governments to influence land and housing markets for the benefit of all, but the poor in particular. For further information on how to achieve this, please load and explore the accompanying CD-Rom. This contains information on how to undertake a livelihoods analysis and a regulatory audit, including a basic matrix which can be adapted to reflect local conditions. It also contains detailed case studies from research in eight countries, plus information on relevant websites and even a game!

ENDNOTES

SECTION 1: REGULATION AND REALITY

1 For more information on this review and the Habitat Agenda, visit UNCHS (2001) 'Habitat Agenda and Istanbul +5', UN-Habitat website: www.unchs.org/unchs/english/hagenda/haghome.htm and UN-Habitat (2003) 'The Habitat Agenda', United Nations Human Settlements Programme website: www.unhabitat.org/declarations/habitat_agenda.asp.

2 Further information and documents related to Agenda 21 can be accessed at UN (2003) 'Agenda 21 – table of contents', UN Department of Economic and Social Affairs, Division for Sustainable Development website: www.un.org/esa/sustdev/documents/agenda21/english/agenda21toc.htm and IISD (1997), 'Agenda 21', International Institute for Sustainable Development website: www.iisd.org/rio+5/agenda/agenda21.htm.

3 Further information on the vision and work of Cities Alliance can be found at Cities Alliance (2003) 'Overview', Cities Alliance website: www.citiesalliance.org.

4 Further information on the Millennium Development Goals and their implementation can be accessed at: 'UN Millennium Development Goals', United Nations website: www.un.org/millenniumgoals/; 'Millennium Development Goals. The global challenge: goals and targets', United Nations Development Programme website: www.undp.org/mdg/; and 'Millennium Development Goals', World Bank Group website: www.developmentgoals.org.

5 Similarly, if something increases by 10 per cent per year, it will double in about seven years. Also, if something increases by 3.5 per cent per year, it will double in about 20 years, and vice versa.

6 See Payne (2001) and Tipple (2003) on the CD-Rom, which suggests that communities should be able to decide collectively on certain standards as long as they do not fall below an agreed threshold.

SECTION 2: REGULATION AND REGULATORY FRAMEWORKS

1 Mayo (1993) emphasized the importance of regulatory reform and audits of housing markets.

2 In this context, prescription indicates something that *must* be done, while proscription is something that must *not* be done.

3 Legal instruments are those based on legislation, while semi-legal instruments may be based on administrative or customary practice.

4 When assessing, reviewing or revising planning regulations and standards, it will be necessary to refer to infrastructure regulations and standards which determine the range and levels of initial and subsequent provision for water supply, sanitation, drainage, power, roads and transportation, and building regulations and standards, which stipulate the quality of construction.

SECTION 3: HOW DO REGULATORY FRAMEWORKS AFFECT THE URBAN POOR?

1 There are exceptions to this rule. For example, in Maseru, the capital of Lesotho, the cost of land remains low, less than 10 per cent of the value of the housing infrastructure in most cases (Hall, 2004).

2 For more information on land tenure and property rights see Payne, 2002a.

3 Sanitation coverage data for urban slum dwellers are not specifically available (UN-Habitat, 2003a, p8).

4 No author (2000) 'Editors' introduction: towards more pro-poor local governments in urban areas'. *Environment and Urbanization* **12**(1): 3–11.

5 Being dependent on specific economic, social, cultural and environmental factors, conditions of adequacy will inevitably vary from one country to another. Adequacy should thus be determined together with the people concerned, taking into consideration possible gradual and continuous development.

SECTION 4: REVIEWING REGULATORY FRAMEWORKS

1   A number of frameworks have been developed. For examples, see Carney et al (1999) and Hussein (2002).
2   How to carry out an SL analysis is described in Section 4 of the DFID Guidance Sheets (DFID, 2000), and is therefore not described in detail in this manual.

SECTION 5: GUIDING PRINCIPLES FOR EFFECTING CHANGE

1   ACHR (no date), 'Expanding poor people's repertoire of learning and teaching tools', Asian Coalition for Housing Rights website: www.achr.net/ffpt3.htm.

REFERENCES AND FURTHER READING

ACHR (Asian Coalition for Housing Rights) (2002) 'Housing by people in Asia. Special issue: community funds', Asian Coalition for Housing Rights, February

Adusumilli, U and Shekdar, D (2004) 'Regulatory guidelines for affordable shelter: the cases of Navi Mumbai and Hyderabad, India', paper prepared for the GPA Regulatory Frameworks for Affordable Shelter Project, available on accompanying CD-Rom

Agarwal, B (1995) *A Field of One's Own: Gender and Property in South Asia*, Cambridge University Press, Cambridge

Ashley, C and Carney, D (1999) *Sustainable Livelihoods: Lessons from Early Experience*, Department for International Development, London

Beall, J (2000) 'Living in the present, investing in the future: household security among the urban poor', in C Rakodi and T Lloyd-Jones (eds) *Supporting Urban Livelihoods*, Earthscan, London

Beall, J and Kanji, N (1998) 'Households, livelihoods and urban poverty' *Urban Governance, Partnership and Poverty* (Working Paper no 3), University of Birmingham, Birmingham

Benjamin, S J (1990) 'Income and housing: understanding household productivity within the framework of urban structuring', in M Rai and P Nientied (eds) *Housing and Income in Third World Urban Development*, Aspect Publishing, London

Benschop, M (2002) 'Rights and realities: are women's equal rights to land housing and property implemented in East Africa?', United Nations Human Settlements Programme, Nairobi

Boonyabancha, S (2003) 'A decade of change: from the Urban Community Development Office to the Community Organisation Development Institute in Thailand' (Working Paper on Poverty Reduction in Urban Areas no 8), International Institute for Environment and Development

Burra, S (2003) 'Changing the rules: guidelines for the revision of regulations for urban upgrading', available on accompanying CD-Rom

Burra, S and Patel, S (2001) 'Norms and standards in urban development: the experience of an urban alliance in India' (paper prepared for the ITDG Regulatory Guidelines for Urban Upgrading Research Project), available on accompanying CD-Rom

Carney, D, Drinkwater, M, Rusinow, T, Neefjes, K, Wanmali, S and Singh, N (1999) 'Livelihoods approaches compared: a brief comparison of the livelihood approaches of the UK Department for International Development (DFID), CARE, Oxfam and the United Nations Development Plan', DFID/IDS, www.livelihoods.org/info/docs/lacv3.pdf

Chambers, R and Conway, G (1992) 'Sustainable rural livelihoods: practical concepts for the 21st century' (Institute of Development Studies Discussion Paper 296), Institute of Development Studies, Brighton

Cities Alliance (2000) 'Making cities work for all: global action plan for city development strategies' (draft) www.citiesalliance.org/fukuoka.nsf/ Attachments/CDS_ActionPlan/$File/ActionPlandraftJune7.pdf

Cohen, M (2002) 'Urban policy and economic development: the agenda', in N Harris (ed) *Cities in the 1990s: The Challenge for Developing Countries*, UCL Press, London

Cotton, A and Tayler, K (2000) *Services for the Urban Poor: Guidance for Policymakers, Planners and Engineers*, Water and Engineering Development Centre, Loughborough University, Loughborough

Davidson, F and Payne, G (2000) *Urban Projects Manual: A Guide to Preparing Upgrading and New Development Projects Accessible to Low Income Groups* (second revised edition), Liverpool University Press, Liverpool

Devereux, S (1999) 'Making less last longer: informal safety nets in Malawi' (IDS Discussion Paper 373), Institute of Development Studies, Brighton

DFID (Department for International Development) (2000) 'Guidance sheets', DFID/IDS, www.livelihoods.org/info/info_guidancesheets.html

DFID (Department for International Development) (2001) 'Sustainable livelihoods guidance sheets', DFID/IDS, www.livelihoods.org/info/ info_guidancesheets.html

FAO (Food and Agriculture Organization) (2002) 'Gender and access to land: land tenure studies 4', FAO, ftp://ftp.fao.org/docrep/fao/ 005/y4308e/y4308e00.pdf

Farrington, J and Oliver, S (2002) 'Drivers for change in Zambian agriculture: defining what shapes the policy environment' (paper prepared for DFID), www.odi.org.uk/Food-Security-Forum/ docs/D4C1.pdf

Hall, D (2004) 'Regulatory frameworks governing access to legal low-income housing in Maseru' (paper prepared for the GPA Regulatory Frameworks for Affordable Shelter Project), available on accompanying CD-Rom

Humphreys, C and Banerji, A (2003) 'World Bank's report on governance and development in MENA region' (paper presented at conference organized by the World Bank and Medea Institute, Brussels, 12 September), Medea Institute, www.medea.be/?doc=1518

Hussein, K (2002) 'Livelihoods approaches compared: a multi-agency review of current practice', DFID/IDS, www.livelihoods.org/info/docs/LAC.pdf

ITDG–EA (Intermediate Technology Development Group–Eastern Africa) (2001) *National Workshop on Regulatory Guidelines for Urban Upgrading*, Lenana Mount Hotel, Nairobi, 8 May (paper prepared for the ITDG Regulatory Guidelines for Urban Upgrading Research Project), available on accompanying CD-Rom

ITDG–EA (Intermediate Technology Development Group–Eastern Africa) (2003) 'The Kenya RGUU experience: context, process and lessons' (paper prepared for the ITDG Regulatory Guidelines for Urban Upgrading Research Project), available on accompanying CD-Rom

Jayaratne, K A, Chularthna, H M U and Premakumra, J (2003) 'Study on regulatory guidelines for urban upgrading: implementation of participatory regulatory guidelines for urban upgrading in Colombo city and secondary towns in Sri Lanka', available on accompanying CD-Rom

Kellett, P W and Tipple, A G (2000) 'The home as workplace: a study of income-generating activities within the domestic setting'. *Environment and Urbanization* **12**(1): 203–13

Kironde, L (2004) 'Regulatory guidelines for affordable shelter: the case of Dar es Salaam, Tanzania' (paper prepared for the GPA Regulatory Frameworks for Affordable Shelter Project), available on accompanying CD-Rom

Lall, S (2001) 'Settlements of the poor and guidelines for urban upgrading: case study of Alwar, a secondary town' (paper prepared for the ITDG Regulatory Guidelines for Urban Upgrading Research Project), available on accompanying CD-Rom

Lowe, L and Schilderman, T (2001) 'The impact of policies, institutions and processes in urban upgrading' (paper prepared for the ITDG Regulatory Guidelines for Urban Upgrading Research Project), available on accompanying CD-Rom

McLeod, R (2001a) 'Costs associated with accessing legal shelter for low-income groups of new urban developments' (paper prepared for the Geoffrey Payne and Associates Regulatory Frameworks for Affordable Shelter Project, May) available on accompanying CD-Rom

McLeod, R (2001b) 'Experiences of linking community-based housing finance to formal finance mechanisms' (paper presented at the Gavle Housing Finance Seminar sponsored by UNCHS and the Swedish Ministry of Housing, March, Gavle, Sweden)

McLeod, R (2001c) 'Humpty Dumpty, poverty and urban governance: an exploration of investment partnerships with the poor' (paper presented at the 2nd Regional Caribbean Meeting of the UNCHS Urban Management Programme, Roseau, Dominica, 19–21 September),

www.theinclusivecity.org/downloads/HumptyDumpty,PovertyAndUrbanG
overnance.PDF

McLeod, R (2001d) 'The impact of regulations and procedures on the livelihoods and asset base of the urban poor: a financial perspective' (paper prepared for the ITDG Regulatory Guidelines for Urban Upgrading Research Project, May), available on accompanying CD-Rom

McLeod, R (2002), 'Research on bridging the finance gap in housing and infrastructure and the development of CLIFF' (interim paper), www.makingcitieswork.org/files/docs/CitiesAlliance/CLIFFbackground.doc

McLeod, R (2003) 'Guidelines for the revision of regulations for urban upgrading: insights from the Federation Process' (paper prepared for the ITDG Regulatory Guidelines for Urban Upgrading Research Project, September), available on accompanying CD-Rom

Majale, M (2002a) 'Regulatory guidelines for urban upgrading: towards effecting pro-poor change', available on accompanying CD-Rom

Majale, M (2002b) 'Towards pro-poor regulatory guidelines for urban upgrading: a review of papers presented at the International Workshop on Regulatory Guidelines For Urban Upgrading, held at Bourton-on-Dunsmore, May 17–18, 2001' (paper presented at the International Workshop on Regulatory Guidelines for Urban Upgrading, 14–16 January, Nairobi), available on accompanying CD-Rom

Mayo, S (1993) 'Housing: making markets work' (World Bank Policy Paper, Washington, DC)

Moser, C (1987a) 'Women, human settlements, and housing: a conceptual framework for analysis and policy-making', in C Moser and L Peake (eds) Women, Human Settlements and Housing, Tavistock, London

Moser, C (1987b) 'Mobilization is women's work: struggles for infrastructure in Guayaquil, Ecuador', in C Moser and L Peake (eds) Women, Human Settlements and Housing, Tavistock, London

Payne, G (2001) 'The impact of regulation on the livelihoods of the poor' (paper presented at the International Workshop on Regulatory Guidelines for Urban Upgrading, 17–18 May, Bourton-on-Dunsmore), available on accompanying CD-Rom

Payne, G (ed) (2002a) Land, Rights and Innovation: Improving Tenure Security for the Urban Poor, ITDG Publishing, London

Payne, G (2002b) 'Lowering the ladder: regulatory frameworks for sustainable development', in D Westendorff and D Eade (eds) Development and Cities, Oxfam, Oxford

Payne, G (2003) 'Getting ahead of the game: a twin track approach to improving existing slums and reducing the need for future slums' (paper presented at the Second World Bank Urban Research Symposium: Urban Development for Economic Growth and Poverty reduction, 15–17 December, Washington DC)

Schilderman, T (2002) 'Strengthening the knowledge and information systems of the urban poor', Intermediate Technology Development Group, www.itdg.org/html/shelter/docs/kis_urban_poor_report_march 2002.doc

Schilderman, T and Lowe, L (nd) 'Regulatory issues affecting shelter development by the urban poor' (second draft, paper prepared for the ITDG Regulatory Guidelines for Urban Upgrading Research Project), available on accompanying CD-Rom

Schilderman. T and Lowe, L (2002) 'The impact of regulations on urban development and the livelihoods of the poor' (paper prepared for the ITDG Regulatory Guidelines for Urban Upgrading Research Project), available on accompanying CD-Rom

SEVANATHA–Urban Resource Centre (2001) 'Regulatory guidelines for urban upgrading: case study of Colombo, Sri Lanka' (paper prepared for the ITDG Regulatory Guidelines for Urban Upgrading Research Project), available on accompanying CD-Rom

Silayo, E (2002) 'Searching for reliable low-cost cadastral survey methods' (paper presented at Workshop on the Regulatory Framework for Affordable Shelter, 12 February, Tanzania)

Singh, V and Kowale, G P (2000) 'Employment conditions, exploitation, safety, income in home-based enterprises in the brassware industry of Aligarh' (paper presented at the CARDO International Conference on Housing, Work and Development: The Role of Home-based Enterprises, 26–28 April, University of Newcastle upon Tyne)

Tayler, K and Cotton, A (1993) *Urban Upgrading: Options and Procedures for Pakistan*, Water, Engineering and Development Centre, Loughborough University of Technology, Loughborough

Tipple, G (2001) 'The impact of regulations on the livelihoods of people living in poverty' (paper prepared for the International Workshop on Regulatory Guidelines for Urban Upgrading, 17–18 May, Bourton-on-Dunsmore), available on accompanying CD-Rom

Tipple, A G (2003) 'What do we learn about regulations from users of housing in developing countries? experience from transformations and home-based enterprises' (paper prepared for the ITDG Regulatory Guidelines for Urban Upgrading Research Project), available on accompanying CD-Rom

Tipple, A G, Coulson, J and Kellett, P W (2002) 'The effects of home-based enterprises on the residential environment in developing countries', in S Romaya and C Rakodi (eds) *Building Sustainable Urban Settlements: Approaches and Case Studies in the Developing World*, ITDG Publishing, London

Turner, J F C (1990) 'Barriers, channels and community control', in D Cadman and G Payne (eds) *The Living City: Towards a Sustainable Future*, Routledge, London

UNCHS (United Nations Centre for Human Settlements (Habitat)) (1996) *An Urbanizing World: Global Report on Human Settlements*, Oxford University Press, Oxford

UNCHS (United Nations Centre for Human Settlements (Habitat)) (1997) *The Istanbul Declaration and Habitat Agenda*, United Nations Centre for Human Settlements (Habitat), Nairobi

UN-Habitat (2001) *Cities in a Globalizing World: Global Report on Human Settlements 2001*, Earthscan, London

UN-Habitat (2002) 'The global campaign on urban governance' (abstract of UN-Habitat concept paper, second edition, Municipal Association of Nepal), www.muannepal.org/resource-center/VoC/VOC_vol3no3/global_campaign.pdf

UN-Habitat (2003a) *The Challenge of Slums: Global Report on Human Settlements 2003*, Earthscan, London

UN-Habitat (2003b) *Water for Cities*, issue 13, pp1, 6, UN-Habitat: www.unchs.org/documents/WAC%20Issue%2012.pdf

UN-Habitat (nd) 'Water and sanitation in the world's cities', UN-Habitat: www.unchs.org/mediacentre/documents/wwf5.pdf

Vanderschueren, F, Wegelin, E and Wekwete, K (1996) *Policy Programme Options for Urban Poverty Reductions: A Framework for Action at the Municipal Level*, World Bank, Washington, DC

World Bank (1999) *World Development Report, 1999/2000: Entering the 21st Century*, World Bank, Washington, DC

World Bank Group (2003) 'Millennium Development Goals', Target 11, www.developmentgoals.org/Environment.htm#target11

Yahya, S, Agevi, E, Lowe, L, Mugova, A, Musandu-Nyamayaro, O and Schilderman, T (2001) *Double Standards, Single Purpose: Reforming Housing Regulations to Reduce Poverty*, ITDG Publishing, London

Index